BODYSCOPES

BODYSCOPES

*Your guide
to how body structure
reveals the secrets of personality*

CAROL SALTUS

BANTAM BOOKS
TORONTO · NEW YORK · LONDON · SYDNEY · AUCKLAND

BODYSCOPES
A Bantam Book / November 1986

Cover and inside illustrations by Garnett Henderson.

Library of Congress Cataloging-in-Publication Data

Saltus, Carol.
  Bodyscopes : your guide to how body structure reveals
the secrets of personality.

  1. Personality.   2. Somatotypes—Psychological
aspects.   3. Personality assessment.   I. Title.
BF698.S228   1986   155.2'64   86-47571
ISBN 0-553-34340-8

Published simultaneously in the United States and Canada

PRINTED IN THE UNITED STATES OF AMERICA
BP   0 9 8 7 6 5 4 3 2 1

To
Elinor Chapple Saltus

Contents

PART
I

WHO AM I?

I.
INTRODUCTION

Do you know who you are? Not: Do you have a set of labels to hand out—"I'm a middle-income, single-parent lawyer"—by which other people can conveniently classify you. But: Do you live with an inner awareness of yourself that is satisfying to *you*; a deep, confident consciousness of your identity?

Many of us grow up without ever finding out who we are. Haunted by a vague but unhappy sense of unreality, we never seem to come into full possession of our true selves—whatever that "self" is. We lose precious years feeling lost, confused, conflicted, afraid that our lives are slipping away from us. We make crucial choices and decisions almost at random, by chance, with the result that for no good reason we may find ourselves marking time in a dead-end job or becalmed in a marriage that we knew was wrong from the outset. It's almost as though we're living someone else's life. How often do we inwardly cry, "What am I doing? How did I get here? How have I let this happen to me?"

This desperate sense of alienation is nothing new, of course.

Over the past quarter-century a bewildering array of treatments for it has sprung up: psychoanalysis, group therapy, family therapy, behavioral therapy, transactional analysis, primal scream, sensitivity training, Gestalt, bioenergetics, Arica, Synanon, not to mention the smorgasbord offered at Esalen. Yet while these therapies provide some relief for some people, they don't provide an answer—and so the search goes on.

But maybe we've gone off in the wrong direction in our search for the self. Is it possible that we've been overlooking the obvious? Most psychotherapies begin—and end—with the mind, with analyzing thoughts and feelings. What if instead we took the body as our starting point? For a century now we've assumed that the individual body has nothing significant to tell us about the mind it houses. From its earliest days, psychoanalysis has ignored the body altogether, as though consciousness were completely independent of it, as though the body were only a sort of incidental container for the intellect and emotions. More recent therapies, such as bioenergetics and Gestalt, have tried to introduce body awareness as an aspect of treatment, but they, too, have paid no attention to the specific body of each individual. "Let the body speak; it tells no lies," these therapists like to say; but they usually mean just that: *the* body, some composite shape talking in a monotone. They, too, are deaf to the voice of the particular structure they see before them—whether it be long and thin, soft and round, or hard and muscular.

And yet we are not disembodied minds; and if we ignore the factor of physical structure, we can never achieve more than a pitifully limited knowledge of ourselves. We don't live from the neck up only; we are our whole selves, body and mind. Not until we learn to put them back together can we discover who we really are.

For centuries it was taken for granted that the body had a lot to say about the kind of person who lived in it; that, in fact, human bodies, with their innumerable variations in structure and shape, were a manifestation of the varieties of personality. The unity of body and behavior was called the *constitution*, those parts of the self that "stand together," and the bodily structure was understood as an expression of the fixed or static aspect of the constitution, of which personality was the dynamics.

The ancients knew this; from Hippocrates on, physicians had noticed that physique and susceptibility to disease were somehow related—that, for example, muscular, athletic people were often vulnerable to heart disease and stroke, while thin people were more inclined to respiratory infections. Somewhat later, body type was linked with the emotions, in the theory of humors: Physique was supposed to be an indication of what kind of bodily fluids predominated, which in turn determined temperament. This theory lives on today as endocrinology, the study of hormones and the ways in which they influence our behavior.

Novelists, painters, and playwrights have always portrayed character as much through body type as through speech, gesture, or costume. We intuitively know that Hamlet must be thin, and the Wife of Bath plump. Only a few seasons ago drama critics complained when the "Man Who Came to Dinner" was incarnated by a tall, thin actor. We expect misers and fanatics to be skinny, and we somehow know that while the most highly sexed people will usually be slim and serpentine (think of the silent movie femmes fatales, such as Gloria Swanson), the cravers of affection, the "love addicts," tend more often to be soft and curvy (Marilyn Monroe). The happy-go-lucky, optimistic world embracers are usually round or square (Sancho Panza, Dr. Watson, Lou Costello, Wally Shawn), while the anxious seekers and questioners are long and lean (Don Quixote, Sherlock Holmes, Bud Abbott, Andre Gregory). Loners are lanky; gregarious people tend to be well-upholstered.

And of course it's very natural for us to make this intuitive link between the inner disposition and the outer form—for the most striking thing about us human beings is our diversity. No other species of the animal kingdom exhibits such an exuberant range of sizes and shapes. Does it make sense to suppose that the equally immense differences among us in our drives and desires, in our relationship to the big issues in our lives—work, play, love, power—are unrelated to our varieties of physical structure?

What made us lose sight for so long of this obvious clue to our inner selves was, paradoxically, a medical victory—the discovery of the environmental causes of disease. For over a century, beginning with Pasteur's great discoveries in the 1870s of the bacterial sources of infection, medicine was concerned mainly with the organisms that invade the body from outside. In the stampede toward all-encompassing environmental explanations, man was reduced, as an anthropologist pointed out, "to an aggregate of millions of wretched cells attacked by other and nastier cells. . . . Man as a total organism went . . . completely out of focus."

But today, medicine is taking another look at constitutions, at wholes, now that the diseases that refused to yield up their secrets to environmental explanations have moved to the forefront as the major killers and cripplers: heart disease, cancer, arthritis, diabetes. Once again doctors are recognizing that body type is a significant factor in both vulnerability and resistance to disease. The American Heart Association lists body type as one of the thirteen risk factors in heart disease— while another body type actually protects against it. Alcoholism is closely associated with a certain body type, depression with another, anxiety states with yet a third. That there is an innate structural tendency toward obesity is now universally recognized by diet experts, who have come to realize that each body type requires its own distinctive approach to weight control—which is why no single diet and exercise plan works for everyone.

In the long history of body typing, or constitutional medicine, one name stands out above the rest: William Sheldon, one of the liveliest and most unconventional minds ever to brighten the landscape of American psychology. Sheldon, who died in 1977, left us a legacy whose implications have been largely unexplored and which is just now beginning to come into its own.

Our psychology has always been committed to the idea that we are a blank slate at birth, and that nothing we bring with us into the world is as important as what happens to us after we've entered it. Our psychology has been as exclusively environmental as our physical medicine. But to Sheldon this meant a cruel and dangerous stifling of the voices of our inherent selves. He rebelled against the psychology of his day, finding it thin and superficial. It began out on the periphery of things, with dreams, attitudes, and emotions—with what was remote and secondary. Why not try reversing this unnatural sequence and start by anchoring oneself first on the rock of basic structure, and then proceed from there?

This was to become his life's work. Building on two great European predecessors—Ernst Kretschmer, who did the first scientific classification of body types, and Carl Jung, who contributed the first modern study of personality types (it was he who identified and described "introverts" and "extraverts")—Sheldon created a complete system showing that psyche was rooted in—was in fact an aspect of—constitution, and that a knowledge of body type could reveal the personality within in profound and important ways often overlooked by conventional psychology.

First, analyzing the human physique, Sheldon found three basic components of structure, all of them present in varying degrees in everyone: endomorphy (*endo* for short), the component of roundness; mesomorphy (or *meso*), the component of muscularity; and ectomorphy (or *ecto*), the component of length. Next he showed that these structural components are linked with traits of temperament; that endo in the physique means relaxation, warmth, and sociability in the personality; meso (pronounced "mez-o") in the physique means energy, assertiveness, and drive in the personality; and ecto in the physique means quickness, sensitivity, and inwardness in the personality.

What counts most, though, is not so much each component considered separately as how they combine to form the person and the personality. All three components are present in every physique, and every psyche, in varying amounts; usually one is dominant, another secondary, and the third the least of the three—although never wholly absent. And it's the blending of these ingredients in their various proportions that gives each of us his or her own particular style of thinking, feeling, and acting.

Sheldon's achievement has provided us with a powerful new tool for self-knowledge, an indispensable key to unlocking the secrets of the self. As Dr. George Sheehan, the runner's guru and longtime Sheldon enthusiast, says, "My body shows me what I am free to be. It does not set a boundary but shows me a fulfillment. And liberates me from a depressing past and an impossible future."

II.
ENDO, MESO, ECTO

READING THE BODY

Who we are is plainly written for anyone to see. Nothing important about us is hidden. Our strengths, our weaknesses, our needs, our fears, our desires—all are immediately visible to anyone who knows how to look.

Our bodies tell our stories. Reading them is a fascinating game, which you can learn to play wherever you see people: in your family, among your friends and lovers, at work, on the street, in the news. Meeting people for the first time, you'll be able to size them up with uncanny accuracy; you will understand things about them at sight that may have puzzled their nearest and dearest for years.

It all begins with the body, and you can learn to read the body like a map. You'll learn a new language, too, both simple and descriptive, a shorthand guide. Soon you and your friends will be able to say:

"I had lunch with the new vice-president today."

"You did! What's he like?"

"Well, I don't know how he'll get along with Lou—he's an

ecto meso." And instantly you'll have a distinct picture of a
certain kind of person—just as when someone says, "You'd
like my brother; he's an Aries too," a specific image springs to
mind.

To read the body, we start by identifying each separate
component of body structure. Then we'll see what the
corresponding components of personality are, and how body
and personality are linked, each reflecting the other. Finally,
we'll see how these basic components of body structure and
personality blend to create the individual physique and the
temperament that matches, and inhabits, it.

First, a silhouette of the body:

Endo: soft, round, cushioned. Endo bodies are centered
around the belly and hips. Endo means plumpness and
curves, short arms and legs, small bones.

Meso: hard, square, solid. Heavy, massive muscles and
bones. A longer torso than the endo's, with the chest
dominant over the belly. Powerful arms and legs.

Ecto: delicacy and decentralization of structure; neither
belly nor chest is dominant. The torso is narrow, flat, and
rather short compared with the long arms and legs. Ecto
stretches the body out, slims and lengthens the bones. (Not
all ectos are tall, however; often they are short, slight people,
but they always have arms and legs that are long in proportion to their bodies.)

Which of these three basic components is dominant in your
body?

If you're soft, round, and curvy, you're an endo; if you're
big-boned and hard-muscled, you're a meso; if you're long-
limbed and slender, you're an ecto.

Having identified the basic components of structure, now
let's take a look at their corresponding traits of temperament.
How do endo, meso, and ecto reveal themselves in personality?

ENDO PERSONALITY:
The Wisdom of the Belly

Endos are belly-centered. The endo component of physique is derived from the inmost layer of the germ cell, which is concerned with nourishment, the most elementary need of organic life—and food is the primary endo pleasure. Endos are slow-moving, calm, and relaxed, because nothing must be allowed to disturb the leisurely process of ingestion and assimilation. Every good thing in life is somehow associated with food. As Lin Yutang, the endo Chinese philosopher, once said, "What is patriotism but love of the good things we ate in our childhood?"

If you're an endo, the peaks of your day are mealtimes; but you have a natural affinity for every kind of ritual gathering together: anniversaries, holidays, class reunions, testimonial banquets—in fact, any social occasion at all. For second only to your love of food is your attachment to people. You hate being hungry, and you hate being alone. Your well-being depends upon a steady flow of emotional support from a group. You cry easily and unashamedly, laugh from the belly, pour out your feelings without restraint. You're emotionally extraverted.

You never lose sight of the fundamentals, of what most concretely and immediately concerns you: maintaining the supply of food and love. You're biologically conservative; you stick close to the earth and your "gut feelings."

Identifying as you do with the group, you tend to be socially and politically conservative. You'll never venture far from established habits and values; you're not a rebel or a revolutionary. So far from wanting to overthrow the existing order of things, you're suspicious of anything that threatens to change any part of it. As one endo put it, "I want this Christmas to be as much like the last as possible." In fact, you resist any change at all. You like comfort, and comfort to you means surroundings that are old and familiar, well loved because well known. Neither adventure nor novelty holds much appeal for you.

You're practical and realistic, with responses that are slow but sure and steady. You don't get flustered easily, or distracted or confused. You take one thing at a time, just as it comes along; nothing can rush or provoke you into rash or hasty action.

You're loving and loyal and sensual, but you're not romantic; you don't long for what's out of sight or reach. You're not a dreamer; there's no glamour for you in a person or thing merely because it's unavailable. You're completely happy with present pleasures—and they're often oral: eating, drinking, smoking, kissing, chatting. You have a limitless curiosity about other people and you love nothing so much as a good gossip, but you're never malicious.

You also get enormous pleasure from sleeping, and your sleep is luxuriously deep and long. You'll never know the meaning of insomnia; the risk is that you'll overindulge in sleep just as you so easily can in food, wallowing in orgies of it.

At a low level of development, endo can mean sloth, gluttony, grossness, and a smothering possessiveness. But, especially if it's balanced by strength in the other two components, endo also means cheerfulness, good sense, stability, a confident and reliable orientation in the world and toward other people. Endo is the component that stands solid as a rock in a crisis, "hanging in." At your best, you radiate geniality, generosity, a glowing good will that draws others to you as to a comforting fireplace. Endo is the component of security, the reservoir of gut strength, of primitive survival; it's our biological insurance against the excesses of meso and ecto.

MESO PERSONALITY:
The Joy of Combat

If the characteristic activity of endos is absorption—of food, warmth, and love—you mesos seek action. You move out assertively into the world; your greatest pleasure is using your muscles to meet and overpower obstacles.

You love a good fight. You're always seeking more challenges to rise to, enemies to defeat. You crave physical adventure the way an endo craves the sensation of a full stomach, and you never stop looking for new worlds to conquer, new ways of exercising your will to power: Almost all athletes and most successful politicians are dominant mesos.

You don't need people the way endos do. You don't mind being alone, and seldom feel lonely—but neither do you crave solitude, as ectos do. Usually you're not particularly aware of whether you're alone or not—although you do like having an audience to witness and applaud your feats. But you never depend upon others for anything essential. You prefer to go out and get—seize—what you want by your own efforts; you enjoy the struggle far more than the possession.

You're emotionally independent, too; if ever you're forced into a passive role, you're acutely unhappy. The harshest punishment that can be inflicted upon you is to make you keep still—and quiet, for you love noise and are naturally noisy, with a loud voice and an explosive laugh. You're happy in an uproar, in your element amid a wall-to-wall blast of sound.

Risk excites you; your instinct is to bet on yourself, on your own courage and skill, in every situation, and you're stimulated by danger. You're boldly direct in going after whatever you want—either brutally so, or with a refreshing lack of guile, depending on one's point of view (victim or admiring bystander). You're ruthless—but not devious, underhanded, or hypocritical; you may lack finesse, but one always knows where one stands with you. You confront every obstacle head-on.

You have tremendous endurance. You need very little sleep and are at your best early in the morning. You mesos are the ones who at sunrise leap joyously out of bed and into an icy shower. Your tolerance for pain is extremely high, and you inflict it without hesitation, although you're not sadistic; you get no kick from the sight of suffering, but neither does it bother you. You're matter-of-fact about pain and indifferent to it—your own or anyone else's.

This trait is one of those great elementary gulfs between people that a knowledge of body type can help to bridge. Endos and ectos often accuse mesos of callousness; once they realize that this insensitivity is not only innate and physiological but that it also goes hand in hand with courage and a capacity for acting cleanly and decisively when others might be too timid or squeamish to do what's necessary, even to save a life—then an enlightened sympathy, or at least tolerance, becomes possible between people who are temperamentally alien.

Body type can tell us a great deal about the range of physiological response. In mesos, the threshold of pain is inherently high. Mesos are the people who refuse anesthesia, not only at the dentist's but sometimes even on the operating table, undergoing minor surgery without painkillers and without flinching. In fact, you may not deserve all the credit you get—and give yourselves—for facing pain bravely, since you don't feel it with the same intensity that other people, especially ectos, do. The great Bronco Nagurski, lineman and fullback for the Chicago Bears, was once, while on a road trip, thrown out of a hotel-room window several floors up by some high-spirited teammates. "The Bronk" landed on his shoulders and back, not only alive but conscious. A crowd gathered and somebody asked, "What's going on?" Replied the Bronk: "I dunno. I just got here."

Where endos are emotionally extraverted, you mesos exhibit extraversion of action. Your feelings and impulses turn immediately into a need to *do* something. You're seldom inhibited by doubt; you decide immediately what to do and swing into action at once.

You're physically expansive in other ways too. You like plenty of space around you, the feeling that your surroundings offer no hindrance to your freedom of movement. You like large rooms with a view opening out to the far horizon (whereas endos like to feel embraced by soft, intimate coziness).

This trait of extraverted action makes it possible for you to move fearlessly in any emergency to meet whatever danger may be approaching. At low levels of development, mesos become the thugs, the bullies, the tyrants. But it's the meso component within us, and the mesos among us, that make possible quick, courageous, and effective action. You mesos are the doers, the executives, the ones who convert dreams into reality.

ECTO PERSONALITY:
The Interior Castle

Endos and mesos are both compact. In endo there's a concentration of mass in the "boiler room," the digestive viscera, while mesos are centered in the "engine room," or chest, the heart-lung power system. But ectos are not centered at all. In ectos there's venturing out into space, with a risky exposure to the enviroment. Ecto is the component of length, and in the ecto body there is a preponderance of surface over volume. Ectos have more skin relative to their total body mass than do either endos or mesos, and since so many nerve endings are in the skin, you ectos are more sensitive and vulnerable to your surroundings. Your sensory feelers are always active, alert to every stimulus, picking up and registering everything going on around you, whether you want to or not.

Where endos are ruled by their bellies and mesos by their muscles, you're dominated by your nervous system. In your temperament, consciousness is king. You're not interested in either ingestion or action; you don't want to *do* anything to your environment. You pay attention to it. Thinking predominates in you over both feeling and movement. And the beam of your attention sweeps inward, through your own sensations and thoughts, as widely as it ranges outward across your environment.

Endos and mesos are extraverts, of emotion and action, respectively; you're the introverts. Restraint and inhibition are your most characteristic physical responses, and what is being inhibited is activity, in the interests of awareness. In contrast with endo relaxation and meso alertness and readiness for action, your ecto body is tense and tight, held in check; physical movement is restrained in you, so that your mind can take the lead.

In this you're likely to be misunderstood by endos and mesos, who don't realize that the tension and the inhibited expression of feeling—which in them would be a sign of trouble—are quite normal for you. They'll see your intense focus on your own mental life as neurotic, but it's instinctive with you to be acutely aware of your internal life.

You're never out of touch with that inner world; it's external reality you're in danger of losing contact with. Because you can never escape the sensation of being nakedly exposed to it, you're usually on somewhat suspicious terms with the outer world. You're especially sensitive to noise. A noise level that an endo or a meso wouldn't even notice may be intolerable to you. The next worst thing is too many people. You have a few close friends, whom you prefer to see one at a time. You're unhappy in crowds, at big parties, in almost any group. If you can't physically escape the crowd, you'll retreat into the realm of your own mind, your "interior castle," where you can find peace and the illusion of control.

With mesos, it's the other way around. Their sense of the world and their own place in it is secure and confident, but they lack self-awareness and are ordinarily cut off from the deeper levels of their own minds. Any sudden crisis in their lives that tears through that tough outer skin, exposing the inner layers of their being, comes as a shock and a revelation. You ectos, ill at ease in the world in so many painful ways, live on familiar terms with shifting levels of interior awareness, with your daydreams and fantasies.

You possess neither the physical strength and endurance of the meso nor the endo's relaxed warmth. You're quick, restless, and impatient; your attention darts about like a bird's. You have a short energy cycle, sleeping lightly, tiring quickly. You're probably a night person. Unlike mesos, you hate getting up in the morning. Your vitality increases as the day wears on, and you're at your best late in the evening; just as the others' eyelids are beginning to droop and they're thinking it's time to go home, yours click open with a sudden thrust of energy.

Because all of your responses are pitched so high and acute, you need more privacy and solitude than most people. In times of trouble or stress, where endos turn for support to others and mesos seek release in action, you need to go off by yourself. To assimilate new experiences, come to terms with a emotional shock or trauma, weigh alternatives in making a difficult decision, or simply to rest and recuperate from overstimulation, you need most of all to be alone with your own thoughts, free from all external pressures.

Since you take in and register so much at once from your environment, you can easily become flustered and confused. Lacking endo and meso insulation of fat and muscle, you respond with your nerve ends to everything that's going on around you. One result of this continuous sensory overload is a more or less permanent nervous apprehensiveness. If you often feel a vague sense of imminent disaster hanging over you like a black cloud, it's probably the ecto in your makeup. Fortunately, it's not always present at full strength. Even the most robust among you are likely to wake up in the morning with a sense of impending doom; but this tends to dissipate as your energy rises later in the day.

Related to this lack of insulation is your extremely low

threshold of pain. You may faint at the sight of blood; you're probably panicked by "needles"; you almost certainly have a highly volatile, suggestible, and easily upset stomach.

Endos and mesos are biologically introverted. They're comfortably centered within themselves at the deeper levels of structure—of gut and muscle, respectively. They compensate for their physiological inwardness by a strong appetite for external stimulation. In trouble they turn outward, to others or to action. You ectos, biologically exposed, are psychological introverts, under stress turning away from the world toward your own internal resources.

Probably you've sometimes wondered what you're doing in the real world at all, you so often feel out of place and uncomfortable in it. You're thin-skinned, high-strung, hypersensitive, irritable, and "antisocial"—but you're also among the longest-lived people. You're highly resistant to most infections, to cardiovascular disorders, and even to cancer. Easygoing endos and powerhouse mesos are likely to be felled without warning in vigorous midlife by strokes and heart attacks; not you frail, a-puff-of-wind-would-blow-you-away ectos. Your fragility seems indestructible.

Another paradox: Neither the sensual endo nor the rippling-muscled meso is any match for you slender, delicate ectos in sexual excitability and passion. Your body can give you a lot of trouble—you never feel quite at home in your skin, you don't look sturdy, and you have little confidence in your ability to perform physically—but to all of these inadequacies, real or imagined, your sexuality is a glorious exception. It's part of your whole pattern of sensual responsiveness—and the same high pitch of arousal means that sex can easily become as much a tormenting obsession as a pleasure. But whether it's pleasure or pain or both at once, sex is never far from your mind.

III.
WHAT'S YOUR
BODY TYPE?

BODY-TYPE CHECKLIST

Here's a checklist of personality traits associated with each of
the three components:

ENDO	MESO	ECTO
Sociable	Independent	Private
Relaxed	Assertive	Tense
Comfort-loving	Physically active	Mentally active
Optimistic	Adventurous	Apprehensive
Generous	Ambitious	Excitable
Practical	Insensitive	Sensitive
Stable	Combative	Passionate
Calm	Bold	Quick

And here's a detailed checklist of the physical traits of each
component:

ENDO

- Large, round head; full, plump face
- Short, soft neck
- High, plump shoulders
- Arms tapering to small wrists, short fingers
- Deep, soft body contours
- Chest widening from top to bottom; belly dominant
- High, deeply curved, hourglass waistline
- Belly rising high on torso
- Large, soft, round buttocks
- Full hips and thighs, tapering to small-boned ankles and feet
- Thighs meet when standing with feet together; strong outer curve along thighs and calves
- Rosy, satiny skin
- Fine-textured hair

MESO

- Large, square head; heavy, massive skull
- Wide, thick neck
- Heavy, sloping shoulders
- Massively muscled chest
- Rugged forearms, with knotty muscles and prominent veins
- No tapering of arms; strong, heavy wrists
- Large, thick, big-knuckled hands and fingers
- Hard, square body contours
- Prominent chest, tapering down to low waistline and small, flat belly
- Long back, with low, sharply indented lumbar curve
- Powerful legs, showing space between thighs when standing
- Thick, deeply creased skin
- Coarse hair; may thin early

ECTO

- Small head, light skull, prominent ears
- Long, slender neck
- Square, thin shoulders; pronounced slump in upper back, head projecting forward
- Prominent shoulder blades
- Long, slender arms, hands, fingers
- Limbs lengthen as distance from center of body increases; forearms longer than upper arms
- Narrow, flat, shallow chest
- High, shallow lumbar curve
- Small, short trunk
- Muscles long, fine, spindly; bony contours dominate over muscle or fat
- Lower legs longer than thighs
- Thin, dry, sensitive skin
- Fine, fairly thick hair

YOUR SINGULAR SELF:
Blending the Elements

The three basic elements are only the beginning. What really matters is how they combine: how round, soft endo; square, hard meso; and long, delicate ecto blend to form the individual body and personality. There are nine body types, each representing a different blend of the three basic components:

Endos:

1. BALANCED ENDO
2. MESO ENDO
3. ECTO ENDO

Mesos:

4. BALANCED MESO
5. ENDO MESO
6. ECTO MESO

Ectos:

7. BALANCED ECTO
8. ENDO ECTO
9. MESO ECTO

Which of these groups is yours?

You already know if you're a dominant endo, meso, or ecto (see page 10). Now, with the help of the accompanying sketches, decide what your secondary component is.

If you're a soft, curvy ENDO:

(1) Are meso and ecto, the components of muscularity and length respectively, about equally present in your physique? Then you're a BALANCED ENDO.

(2) Are your endo curves firmed and shaped by solid underlying muscle? Are you elastically rounded, bouncy rather than soft? Then you're a MESO ENDO.

(3) Are your endo curves stretched out, so that your body is soft, long, and high-waisted, with long limbs and fingers? (Long fingers are a sure sign of ecto.) Then you're an ECTO ENDO.

If you're a heavy-boned, muscular MESO:

(4) Are the lengthening influence of ecto and the softening of endo about equally present in your physique? Then you're a BALANCED MESO.

(5) Is your rugged meso muscularity somewhat smoothed and softened? Is your muscle definition prominent, but sleeked and rounded? And are your arms and legs of average length, or shorter, in comparison with your torso? Then you're an ENDO MESO.

(6) Is your basic strong muscularity lean and wiry? Are you broad-shouldered, with a prominent chest and arms and legs that are long in proportion to the trunk? Then you're an ECTO MESO.

If you're a slender, long-limbed ECTO:

(7) Are endo softening and gentle curving, and meso muscle definition, about equally present in your physique? Then you're a BALANCED ECTO.

(8) Is your long ecto body willowy and loose-jointed, sinuous and soft, high-waisted and a bit round-shouldered? Then you're an ENDO ECTO.

(9) Is your basic ecto length and delicacy of bone given an underlay of long, slender muscles? Are you square-shouldered, with a tapering chest and a slim waist? Then you're a MESO ECTO.

You've found your body type. In Part II, you'll find the Bodyscope for your type.

ENDO MEN

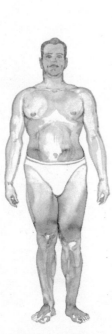

Balanced Endo

Plump shoulders; soft, full, rounded chest; belly rises high on body, waistline high and indented; full, curving hips and thighs; relatively short forearms and calves. A deep, soft body.

Meso Endo

Shoulders broader, squarer, chest heavier than on balanced endo (but still less prominent than belly); the whole surface less smooth, muscle contours much more prominent. A sturdier, more rugged and solid body.

Ecto Endo

Gently curved, as in balanced endo, but the curves are elongated; narrower shoulders and hips, but belly still more prominent than chest, waistline still high; arms and legs longer and more slender. A soft, round, relaxed body that has lengthened out.

24

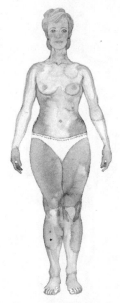

Balanced Endo

Soft, gently swelling curves; full, smooth shoulders; high, hourglass waistline; deeply curved, prominent belly, hips, and thighs. A small-boned, billowy body.

Meso Endo

Much more strongly muscled, the curves more firmly molded and even more pronounced than in the balanced endo; broader shoulders, a more prominent chest, waistline slightly lower; belly, hips, and thighs less soft, the curves more robust and solid throughout.

Ecto Endo

Chest and shoulders narrower than in balanced endo; waistline still high, but less sharply indented; belly and hips narrower, slimmer; arms and legs longer relative to torso. Endo curves have lengthened into slender softness.

25

MESO
MEN

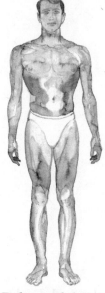

Balanced Meso

Massive chest, strongly dominant over lower torso; shoulders very broad and sloping; small, flat belly; space between thighs. A powerful body, with craggily prominent muscle contours throughout.

Endo Meso

Body slightly less hard and rugged, muscle contours softened and more rounded; chest dominant over belly, but not so overwhelmingly as in balanced meso; waistline slightly higher and thicker; hips slightly broader; belly a little rounder. A compact, sturdy, rugged body.

Ecto Meso

Slimmed and lengthened muscularity; narrower chest, less sharply tapered waist, hips more slender; arms and legs longer, relative to torso. More angular, leaner, and lighter than the other meso bodies.

MESO
WOMEN

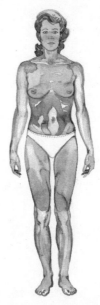

Balanced Meso

Chest and shoulders strongly dominant over belly; low waistline, with little indentation; narrow pelvis and hips; strong arms and legs, no tapering; well-defined muscle contours. A clean-cut, sturdy, athletic body.

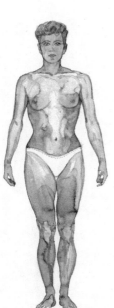

Endo Meso

Chest still distinctly dominant over belly, but the whole body much more curved than in balanced meso; higher and more indented waistline, curvier belly and hips. A compact, rounded, solid body.

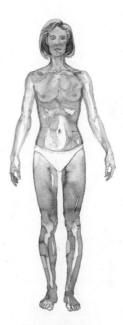

Ecto Meso

Longer and slimmer than balanced meso; more slender, narrower chest and hips; longer arms and legs; the whole body less compact, more lengthened out. A lean, lithe, and agile body.

ECTO MEN

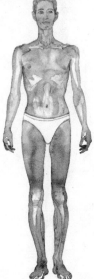

Balanced Ecto

Square shoulders; flat chest; narrow waist, narrow hips; long, slender arms and legs. A sharp, angular, clean-cut body.

Endo Ecto

Angles gently rounded; waistline slightly higher, somewhat rounder belly than in balanced ecto; length is curved and eased, with less bony sharpness. The body is loosened, softened, more relaxed.

Meso Ecto

Deeper, more prominent chest; broader shoulders; less narrow waist than in balanced ecto; muscle contours more rugged throughout. A taut, wiry body.

28

ECTO WOMEN

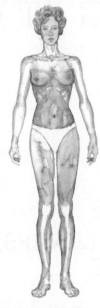

Balanced Ecto

Narrow, shallow, rather short torso; square shoulders; very long, slim arms and legs; narrow hips and pelvis. A light, sharp, alert body.

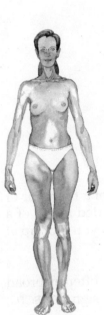

Endo Ecto

Softer, rounder, looser than the balanced ecto; less tapered waistline; belly and hips more curved and prominent. A long, soft, willowy body.

Meso Ecto

Broader, deeper chest, tapering more sharply to the waist than in balanced ecto; arms and legs not quite so long relative to torso; stronger and more pronounced muscle contours throughout. A lean, tense, muscularly slender body.

IV.
LOOKING AT OTHERS

STRANGERS, LOVERS, AND FRIENDS

Sometimes you'd like to know the body type of a friend or of an interesting stranger glimpsed across a crowded room, of a lover or a celebrity in the news. What clues can you pick up at a glance?

- Look at the neck. MESO necks are very broad, often as broad as the head. Long, slender necks are a sign of ECTO; smoothly cylindrical necks are ENDO.

- Shoulders: Broad, sloping shoulders are MESO; narrow, square shoulders are ECTO; high, full shoulders are ENDO.

- Long arms and legs and long, slim fingers are signs of ECTO.

- Wrists and hands: Heavy-boned wrists are a sign of MESO; slender wrists, of ECTO; plump wrists and short fingers, of ENDO. Big veins standing out prominently on forearms and hands mean MESO; so do big knuckles.

- If the body is a massive one, is the mass concentrated in the upper or lower part of the torso; that is, is the waist low or high? If the chest dominates, so that the waist is low on the trunk, it's a MESO body; if the waistline is high, rising almost up to the ribcage, it's an ENDO body.

- Is the contouring of the body's surface smooth and even, or does it show strong muscle definition? If the former, it's an ENDO body. If the latter, are the muscles thick and massive (MESO) or long and sinewy (ECTO)? Or it may be a combination: If the muscle development is strong and hard over limbs that are slender but compact, it's an ECTO MESO body. If the torso, arms, and legs are predominantly long and slim but there is a pronounced muscle definition, it's a MESO ECTO body. If the muscle definition is strongly marked but cushioned and sleeked, it's an ENDO MESO body. If the surface is smooth with muscles just visible beneath the dominant cushioning endo, it's a MESO ENDO body. And if no definition is visible from either muscle or bone, and the body looks both long, soft, and round, it's either an ENDO ECTO or an ECTO ENDO body, depending on whether length or roundness is dominant.

- Sitting: A comfortable sprawl, loose and relaxed, is characteristic of ENDOS; sitting erect, with the head held high, of MESOS; while ECTOS tend to sit slumped, resting on the middle of their backs. (If possible, ECTOS like to have their feet higher than their heads; they're the ones who sit or lie with their feet propped up against a wall or a tree.)

- Walking: ENDOS roll smoothly along, relaxed and easy. A pounding swagger, with the heels hitting hard, is a MESO giveaway (although not every meso walks this way). ECTOS walk with constraint, held in, their arms close to their bodies, sometimes even hugging the chest.

- Voice: ENDO voices are melodious. MESO voices are loud, unselfconsciously penetrating and carrying, with an explosive, pistol-shot laugh. ECTO voices are subdued and quiet, as restrained as their movements.

FAMOUS BODIES

Here are some famous people, grouped according to their dominant component:

ENDOS	**MESOS**	**ECTOS**
Elizabeth Taylor	Ronald Reagan	Audrey Hepburn
Winston Churchill	Bing Crosby	Jean Cocteau
Elvis Presley	Pete Rose	Lucille Ball
Marilyn Monroe	Golda Meir	James Stewart
Luciano Pavarotti	Martina Navratilova	Twiggy
Lowell Weicker	Mario Cuomo	Franz Kafka
Orson Welles	Caroline Kennedy	Nancy Reagan
Shelley Winters	Norman Mailer	Virginia Woolf
Buddy Hackett	Clint Eastwood	Jonathan Miller
Dolly Parton	Margaret Mead	Suzanne Farrell

PART
II

THE
BODYSCOPES

I.
ENDOS:
The People of Feeling

Endos are soft, curvy,
generous, affectionate, and optimistic.
Endos come in three varieties:
balanced endos, meso endos, and ecto endos.

1. BALANCED ENDOS:
Sleek and Curvy

Who You Are

Smooth-sailing, serene, imperturbable: In balanced endos, all
endo traits come through clear and strong. With meso and
ecto at equal but secondary strength below, the endo rises
emphatically over both.

The most obvious thing about you endos is the depth of
your relaxation. Your whole being is loose, easy, slow-
moving, and slow to excite or arouse. You're never rushed,
jerky, or strained; you roll along as through a deep, calm sea,
and wherever you go you exert a soothing, steadying influence.

Everything about you is open, flowing, and free. Your voice
especially is notably pleasant, often beautiful; you have none
of the tension and stridency, the agitation, or the urge to
overpower by sheer volume that so often characterize ecto
and meso voices. You're open, too, in being not only

accessible but welcoming to the whole world. You expect friendliness wherever you go, and you usually meet it in return. You never encounter new people or situations with an attitude of suspicion or withdrawal; you have legions of friends, and to you a strange place is merely a fresh opportunity for making more.

Your inner security allows you to be outwardly trusting, to the dismay of your ecto friends, who are always fearful that you'll be deceived or betrayed—which is what they fear for themselves. But in fact your trust is usually justified, for your equally strong, practical common sense—together with your utter refusal to be rushed into action—saves you from most serious mistakes of judgment. You may look like a softy, but it's surprisingly difficult to take advantage of you.

All of your responses are deliberate and unworried. It's not the superficial "cool" of nerves and emotions reined in; you're genuinely and profoundly tranquil. Physiologically, the component of endo represents the involuntary organ systems of the body, the part of the self that lies deepest within, buried safely beyond reach of all conscious interference, all anxious, irritable prodding or provoking. You can't be readily "got at," and you can never be hurried.

You're naturally inert; only after long reflection will you start moving. You can all too easily become lazy and sluggish. Keeping active is vital for your well-being, and it's easy for you to stay active once you've begun, for above all, you're a creature of habit. The hardest part is overcoming your habitual inertia. Endos who recognize and take advantage of this fact about themselves are the ones who triumph over their tendency to stop moving and put on weight, especially in later adult life; they teach themselves to substitute the habit of activity for that of indolence. (More about this at the end of the chapter.)

When you endos finally do act, it's with a deep inward confidence. You'll never borrow trouble; in whatever you undertake, you expect a happy outcome. A friend of the actor Robert Morley has remarked, "In my view he owes not a little of his success to the facility he has for shrugging off even the threat of failure. To those people who doubted his ability to follow such experts at the game as Noel Coward, Marlene Dietrich and Sophie Tucker and warned him of what might happen to him if he attempted cabaret at the Café de Paris, he replied airily, 'The worst that can happen is that I shall discover I cannot do cabaret at the Café de Paris. It's nothing to be ashamed of. Nor is it something for which I shall be pointed at in the street or forced to leave the country.'"

Although calm and confident, you do tend to be low in aggressive energy and drive. While you will respond, however slowly, you seldom initiate. But your friends and co-workers soon learn, first, that all attempts to hurry or harry you will result only in frayed nerves for them; and furthermore, that your composure in a crisis is usually far more effective than any showy display of assertiveness.

But if you're passive, you also possess a long patience. "Nothing made in haste will last" is the attitude of the great endo craftsmen, who in their eighties and even nineties steadily carry to completion their life's work, leisurely and serene, secure and trusting as ever that they will have all the time they need to finish it.

Consuming Passions

You love food—literally. It's a lifelong romance that goes way beyond physical appetite. To you, food is an endlessly fascinating preoccupation. Mealtime is a ceremony that you approach with reverence. Wherever there's eating, drinking, and conviviality you'll be found: managing hotels, tending bar, working as restaurateurs, chefs, caterers, professional party-givers, like Elsa Maxwell, James Beard, Toots Shor, Julia Child, Elaine. (A restaurant whose owner is low in endo probably offers mediocre food to a clientele of chic dieters.)

If you're not actually in the food business, you will always know, as well as you know the rooms in your house, the restaurants in your neighborhood: their specialties, their hours, whether they deliver, if they're open on Sunday, whether the new management is as reliable as the old, where the chef came from.

You'll happily spend weeks preparing for a party. Christmas begins in August, and you'll seize on any pretext for feasting and celebrating: winning the election or losing it, arriving or departing, a birthday or an unbirthday. No one knows better than you how to have a good time, and your basic good time—the earliest agreeable sensation of organic life—is the pleasure that comes from an excellent digestion; not only eating, but the whole subsequent progress of the food through the body as well. Endos like everything about the experience of assimilation: the full stomach, the digestive rumble, the comfortable belch, even passing wind and elimination. Babies enjoy these sensations and sounds, too, before they've been taught to find them disgusting, and it's characteristic of you endos, in many of your attitudes and values, to keep a channel open back to babyhood.

You take great delight in sleep too. You have no trouble at any time falling instantly into it, deeply and heavily. Winston Churchill used to say, "I look forward to dying. Sleep, endless, wonderful sleep—on a purple velvety cushion. Every so often I will wake up, turn over, and go to sleep again."

Comfort is your aim. Your soft curves luxuriate in overstuffed furniture, beds with downy mattresses you can sink into, plump pillows, thick quilts, deep carpets. (To mesos, who need a lot of space, visiting an endo's house feels like being locked inside a padded velvet jewel box.) Since you're innately conservative, you'll wear tight, constricting clothes if they're in fashion, but you're most unhappy in them. Given the choice, both the men and women among you would prefer always to wear loose, flowing robes, such as caftans and djellabas.

You're traditionalists. You treasure old ways, old customs; your emotional roots sink deep into the past. You enjoy pomp and pageantry, dressing up in quaint costumes and uniforms, parading about in grandiose processions. You resent and resist modernization in all its forms, efficiency that's bought at the price of a cold, mechanical impersonality; high-tech surroundings are not your style.

You are the indefatigable organizers of banquets and benefits, testimonial dinners and fancy-dress charity balls, rock concerts, rummage sales, circuses—anything that brings people together. You love the feeling of being part of a crowd, one among many; you find your identity in union. "Alone is like a stone," and alone might as well be dead. Solitude, which refreshes and restores ectos, frightens you.

You're sometimes accused of snobbishness because you gravitate toward the "important" people, the power brokers, the celebrities and hostesses. It's not power or influence you're seeking, however, but connection. You cultivate the higher levels of the social hierarchy not because the people up there are influential but because they're the center of a network: the source of more people, more connectedness.

Friends are the strongest emotional need of your life, and yours can always count on you. You're solidly dependable; your loves last for years—for life. You're not drawn to the challenge of seducing aloof or inaccessible people, nor are you excited by those who may hurt you; there's no masochism in your makeup. Love is never a power play.

But should you lose a loved one, you'll quickly find a replacement. Not that you don't care deeply about a particular person—but what's vital to you is the role of wife, husband, lover, or confidant, and that somebody be there to occupy that position in your life. Your dread is of the empty space; it's not that you're superficial, but your deepest attachment is to the role rather than the specific person filling it.

It's one aspect of endo conservatism, and a compelling reason for your refusal ever to feel bad about anything for very long. When you've suffered a loss, your grief is whole-hearted and real, but you don't stay sunk in it any longer than you have to. You soon dry your tears and start casting about for a replacement.

Since both breadth and intensity of feeling are rarely found in the same person, you seldom either experience or inspire a narrow, exclusive passion. You're seldom jealous either, because your own affections are not measured quantitatively. You don't parcel yourself out, or take away from one what you bestow upon another. Nor do you value anything solely because someone else doesn't have it. And your friends could no more feel jealously possessive of you than they could resent the sun for not shining on them alone. Miraculously, everyone in your world receives all your love, undivided and all at once.

When trouble strikes, you'll roar with pain, weep floods of tears, shudder with great belly-heaving sobs. You give yourself over wholly to the expression of your misery, which will be noisy but not prolonged. You never cling to grief; your instinct is to purge it—accept it, acknowledge it, and then cast it off. Digest it, and eliminate it.

Under stress—which always reveals what is basic in temperament—you look around for a shoulder to cry on. You instinctively seek to diffuse unhappiness by "sharing" it. The mere presence of sympathetic others is the beginning of healing for an endo in pain, no matter how terrible. You're never the ones who can't wait for everyone to go home and leave you alone with your sorrow; that's an ecto response.

"Go on, have a good cry; get it out of your system" is typical endo advice. Joy, too, is overflowing; you're as generous with your feelings as you are with all your other possessions. And not only are you uninhibited in expressing them, to you feelings are genuine only if and when they are expressed; an emotion repressed is no emotion at all. You consider ectos, who keep their feelings under lock and key, to be cold, detached, unloving. You're uninterested in, and largely unaware of, whatever is hidden or withheld. If it doesn't show, it doesn't exist; the latent or invisible is not real.

What the Eye Doesn't See . . .

The importance of appearance, of surfaces, as a guide to reality is the main source of your love of ritual and ceremony, and of your preoccupation with etiquette. "Take care of the outside, and the inside will take care of itself" is the endo motto. Good manners mean more than inward disposition— or rather, they determine it. Because you hide nothing yourself, you have little awareness of hypocrisy, and never suspect that there may be a discrepancy between what someone exhibits to the world and what he "really" feels. "Outward show" *is* inward truth; for you, there's never any split between them.

And it's true that with most people, most of the time, the

surface *is* an accurate guide to the inside. But not always; and whenever it's not, endos are likely to be out of their depth. For example:

Sam, a jovial endo, and Tony, a high-strung meso ecto, worked on the same weekly newsmagazine, Tony as the literary editor and Sam in the advertising department. After a devastating three-year illness, Tony's wife died. The long, losing battle to save her wore him out, and a few days after the funeral, depression overwhelmed him like an ocean tide. Now Tony had a new fight on his hands, against these waves of blackness. As long as he had the office to look forward to the next day, he could just manage the evenings, but weekends were dangerous. His friends were worried about him.

Late one Saturday afternoon Sam was having drinks with friends at a bar when it suddenly occurred to him he was only a couple of blocks from Tony's house. He called him up and asked him to come out and join the crowd. Tony was not in the mood for any crowd, but Sam pressed him and finally Tony invited him to drop by the house alone later.

Tony had a good supply of Scotch, and Sam had some hot gossip from the office that Tony, in his abstracted withdrawal, hadn't heard. A love affair had ignited between one of the editors and a woman from the art department, and there was lots to speculate about: her husband, his wife, the editor in chief, who had caught them actually "at it" in a conference room during lunch hour. "You open a closet at your peril these days; you reach for your coat, and Vince and Linda fall out on top of you from between the hangers." It was a juicy story, and Sam, a talented raconteur, made the most of it.

Before they knew it, it had gotten too late to go out to eat, but Tony, who had learned to cook back when Lorraine first fell ill, fixed them a substantial dinner: steak, salad, baked potato, even cheesecake with raspberries for dessert. They ate it companionably in front of the television set, watching a basketball game. Exactly Sam's idea of a pleasant evening. Around one in the morning Tony poured him a nightcap and Sam headed happily for home, completely reassured about Tony: "He's doing great."

Closing the door behind Sam, Tony turned off the television, put the Scotch and brandy back in the liquor cabinet, carried the remains of dinner back to the kitchen, wrapped up the leftovers and stashed them in the refrigerator, washed the dinner dishes, dried them and put them away, went into the bedroom, undressed, hung up his clothes in the closet, put on his pajamas, opened the handkerchief drawer in his dresser, took out an army Colt .45, went into the bathroom, closed the door, pushed the barrel into his mouth, and pulled the trigger.

When he heard the news Monday morning, Sam was stunned and stupefied. What had he done wrong? What should he have done? What did he miss?

Because Tony was capable of going through the motions, Sam accepted them at face value. What he failed to perceive was how distant Tony was, how mechanically and remotely he performed the ritual gestures of hospitality. The fact that he *did* perform them was enough for Sam; caught up in his own spell as an entertainer, he was oblivious to the robotlike quality of Tony's responses. If Tony had sent up broad distress signals, the sort Sam himself would have emitted—desperate weeping, refusal to eat or drink (always, to any endo, a sign of dire emergency)—he never would have left Tony alone that night. But Tony, skilled like all ectos at hiding his feelings, and intent that particular evening on concealing his despair from Sam, succeeded only too well.

The Eternal Moment

Endos live contentedly in a continuous present, serenely flowing with the flow of time, knowing neither regret for the past nor apprehension of the future. All those therapies that flourished in the 1960s and 1970s whose aim was to induce people to live in the "here and now"—which was to be achieved through various techniques of relaxation, body centeredness, and loving physical contact with others—were meant to heighten the influence of endo, in the individual and the world. And certainly, if one is not a dominant endo, one of the most effective strategies for combating the psychic and physical stress of anxiety is to call upon the endo component within oneself.

To you endos, worry and dread are alien emotions, imply-
ing as they do fears about the future; your faith knows that
"sufficient unto the day." Your joys are all of the present
moment: a kiss, a hug, a song, a good meal, a good gossip,
even the warmth of sunshine or the caress of a cool breeze.
"Present mirth hath present laughter": every sensual joy is
immediate.

Nor are you much given to nostalgia, wistfully looking back
to a vanished past, a lost childhood. You don't need to—
you're the great rememberers; to you nothing is ever lost.
Your loyalty to tradition sees to it that the past is carried into
the present with undiminished radiance. Never do you
overlook a birthday or an anniversary, and you're fierce about
preserving every detail of the sacred rituals, vigilant against
the slightest innovation or deviation from "the way we always
do it": the special Christmas chocolate cake, from a recipe that
goes back five generations in Budapest; the honeymoon hotel
faithfully revisited every year through the golden anniversary,
"our room" with the balcony, the yellow roses, the champagne and candlelight.

You seize every opportunity to inaugurate new rituals too.
An impromptu trip to the lake upstate one Fourth of July
immediately becomes the traditional annual Fourth of July
family picnic. Anyone who dares suggest, "Let's do something different this year," gets a shocked stare in return, as if
they were proposing to monkey around with the Mass.

In your deep conservatism, your virtual worship of the
aristocracy of old families, you're drawn not toward status,
but continuity. You cling to ancestral heirlooms; no stainless
steel or Plexiglas furniture for you, but wood polished satiny
from generations of use. Home is a nest of memories, of the
objects that define a life: old photograph albums, dried
flowers, seashell collections from childhood summers at the
shore, bits of Venetian glass, English silver, French china,
souvenirs of long-ago travels, old sheet music. You love songs
and have an extensive repertoire of the old ones, which carry
such a freight of feeling.

(Many of these endo traits are of course the ones associated
with femininity. But actually it's the endo in their makeup that

elicits these tendencies in women. Among men in whom endo is high, one finds the same sentimental attachments to old things and ways, the same need for frequent gestures of affection and appreciation, the same "maternal" instinct for taking care of people.)

You're constant in your everyday habits, too, as loyal to these as to everything else in your life. The rhythms of your biological cycle are slow, deep, and regular. Energy flows evenly and steadily, with no abrupt highs and lows, no shocks or surprises. Some of your colleagues and co-workers may at first see you as slow and plodding, but they soon learn to value the efficiency of your placid, unflustered pace in achieving any objective. A surge of speed that's immediately paid for by a drastic falling back, the irregular, jagged rhythms of more "dynamic" but erratic people may look spectacular during the highs of activity, but the lows can last twice as long as the highs. You may be undramatic, but you come through.

Another advantage you offer to the working world is your undistractibility. If you're slow, you're also single-minded, pursuing your goal with dogged determination, inexorably, and like the drop of water that wears away stone, in the long run better at getting the job done than the more conspicuously energetic types. With your strong sense of responsibility, you always meet deadlines, allowing plenty of time to get the job done properly, never delaying until it's too late to do it right. Pressure is never a spur to your best performance; you know better than to take on rush jobs.

Although a disproportionate number of you endos make the dean's list and Phi Beta Kappa, your intellect tends not to be probing or analytical. It's most often firmly grounded in sensory reality, little inclined to theory or abstraction, or to extreme subjectivity. You're unlikely to become an elementary particle physicist, a mathematician, a research chemist, or a lyric poet; more likely to be a novelist, an historian, a painter, a chef. You're makers, synthesizers, rather than dissecters or demolishers. Such people are concerned with clearing away the old to make way for the new; your instinct is to preserve the old against the assaults of the innovators.

The whole purpose and meaning of life for you is social

communion, and almost all your activity is in some way directed to that end. In any business, you're the indispensable collaborator rather than the lone individualistic entrepreneur. Your talents are cooperative. You shine at weaving a fruitful working partnership among people with a high coefficient of friction who would be incompatible, warring elements without your emollient presence. Your tranquillity oils the wheels, smooths the path of the more excitable, abrasive self-starters. A wise meso executive will get you, his endo partner, to do the firing; you can make the victim feel that the company's loss is his gain, and that it's in his own best interests to move on.

"The Sweetness of Flowing Water"

Your sexuality, especially the way the rest of us imagine the women among you, is full of contradictions. On the one hand, we perceive you as nourishing, sheltering, consoling mothers. From this point of view, you're permitted only a passive sexuality; you're expected to serve as a safe harbor from the storms of lust. But then there's the puritanical vision of endos as embodying all the sins of the flesh; as lewd, grossly lascivious, the prey of uncontrollable appetites, voracious of sex as of food (the latter as metaphor for the former was the point of the famous eating scene in the movie *Tom Jones*).

Such an attitude is more common in the Protestant North; the Mediterranean South has an entirely different feeling about luxuriant female flesh—one that suffuses, for example, the films of Fellini. He loves and admires fat women much as did Rubens, whose nudes, as the critic Kenneth Clark pointed out, "never pause to calculate material advantage or nurse an unacted desire. They have the sweetness of flowing water. . . . They are grateful for life, and their gratitude spreads all through their bodies."

A sunny sensuality that pervades the whole self like breathing is far more characteristic of endo sexual feelings than a sharp urgency. It's part of your exuberant enjoyment of everything about the body, and what you crave is contact. You love fondling, caressing, hugging, kissing, cuddling in big double beds. You need a lot of loving reassurance from others, and you eagerly return it. Your sexuality is diffused over your entire body; sex is far more an occasion for stroking and being stroked than for penetration. Extravert here as everywhere else, you need the stimulation of the surface, the skin, more than any internal sensations.

One of your most endearing qualities is your relative indifference to whether you're giving or receiving. An atmosphere of genial plenty is the main thing—never mind who's providing it. Your temperament is most intimately linked with the period of development before the establishment of boundaries, of the separate, isolated, selfish ego. While you love getting presents, it's never because of their intrinsic value. A bunch of flowers can mean as much as a diamond bracelet; what counts is the feeling behind it—above all, that it's a sign the giver continues to be receptive to the rich outpouring of your bottomless affection.

Loving the Whole Self

Curbing the curves is the main concern of any health program for endos. Not getting rid of them; not taking a broomstick or a Twiggy as your ideal; but striking a balance between a *healthy* expression of your innate endo, and obesity. You should never strive to be skinny, but neither need you permit yourself to balloon out of control.

The health hazards associated with obesity are well documented. Obese people are far more likely than those of normal weight to suffer from adult-onset diabetes. They're highly susceptible to gall bladder trouble and to joint disorders—the weight-bearing joints in the small-boned endo frame, hyperflexible to begin with, can be severely damaged by the stress of carrying excess weight. And hypertension (high blood pressure) is particularly dangerous in the obese. Both diabetes and hypertension are important risk factors in cardiovascular disease and stroke. There's a relationship, too, many doctors believe, between obesity and the risk of breast cancer.

Since you endos are naturally easygoing, with a slow pulse, slow metabolism, and slow reaction time, relatively little of what you consume is expended in maintenance or activity. You have an innate tendency, therefore, to put on weight. But being an endo does *not* mean being doomed to fatness. You have the *potential*—the talent, so to speak—for becoming fat, but like all talents this one need not be fully developed. Of all the components, endo is the most fluid in its expression; as an endo, you can stay slender all your life, if you want to and will work at it.

For most of you endos, the desirable weight is *not* bone-thin. Not all bodies can be both thin and healthy, or thin and beautiful. "The question each woman has to answer for herself is: How fat is too fat?" says restaurant critic Mimi Sheraton. Her own answer was influenced by "the drawings of Petty and Vargas that appeared in *Esquire* magazine during my youth, by the value men obviously placed on women with large bosoms (the classic heroines of that era being Ann Sheridan, the 'oomph' girl, and Lana Turner, *the* sweater girl). There was also the voluptuousness of the small waists, round hips, high breasts, and dimpled cleavage induced by the boned and laced corselet known as a Merry Widow. . . .

"I was conditioned then to a certain softness in women, rather than to the angular boniness now fashionable, and being soft and curvaceous was ever my aim. Fortunately, there have always been more than enough marvelous men around who seemed to agree with me."

At last, after a tyranny of the skinny that has ruled fashion for over a generation, the tide seems to be flowing back the other way. Dr. Hilde Bruch, an authority on eating disorders, has remarked, "It is an amazing paradox that our culture, with its great flexibility and liberal ideas, attempts to superimpose *one* form of body build on those whom nature has endowed differently." Perhaps we're becoming more accepting of differences. Or perhaps it's the fitness craze that has paved the way for a new appreciation of the beauty inherent in every variety of healthy body structure, not just one version of it. Even *Vogue* magazine has decreed, "Every body is most beautiful at its healthy weight. Appealing plumpness is not obesity."

The success or failure of any weight control program for

endos is bound up with accepting yourself *as* an endo. The problem is never getting the weight off; it's keeping it off. You can lose weight on any diet, although crash diets are the least effective in the long run. The faster the weight comes off, the sooner it tends to creep back on again—mainly because the loss hasn't been gradual enough to enable you to develop permanent new eating habits while you were dieting. Going on "maintenance" then means going right back to your old ways.

The endos who yo-yo from one fad crash diet to the next are usually people whose attitude toward their bodies dooms them to defeat. If you're motivated by self-disgust; if, in a spasm of loathing for your endo self, you plunge into a masochistic regime of semistarvation that amounts to self-mutilation but promises that you can get rid of ten pounds of your despised flesh in ten days—then you've virtually guaranteed yourself failure. Endos who are successful in combating obesity do it out of love for their *whole* self, not out of anger or hate.

Says Eda LeShan, an endo psychotherapist: "In the course of my long struggle, I tried to deal with every possible aspect of my problem—my heredity, my childhood and adolescence, my adulthood. By the time I finally found the right diet and was able to stick to it, I had discovered that none of all this groundwork could pay off—I couldn't really be ready—*until I had learned to love myself fat.* I had identified the enemy—and the enemy was me. Ultimately, readiness is a personal affirmation; not the fear of dying, not shame or guilt, but finding oneself lovable—and worthy of care."

Well-being for Balanced Endos

Becoming Your Best Self

One happy result of accepting your endo self from the outset is that you become gentler with respect to your eventual goal. Instead of rejecting wholesale *all* roundness, *all* curves, all the other appealing qualities of endo that go along with the fatness, you now aim at becoming your best *endo* self—slimmer, but with a more ample body than your former ideal, not an impossibly long-limbed stick figure.

A crucial factor is the support—or lack of it—that you receive from others. Here are two cases in point:

Esther, the campus beauty, married George, the college football star, immediately after graduation. At twenty, Esther was all slender curves; her body had no angles but also gave no hint of what was to come. Today, at forty-three, after three children, Esther is sixty pounds heavier.

George has long since stopped taking her out. He calls her Fatso, and almost refuses to look at her. "He can't stand me because I don't weigh exactly what I did when we went on our first date. I think he'd like to see me on a permanent diet of coffee and fingernails. Does everybody *have* to be thin?"

One problem is that George married a status object, not a real woman with a real body that changes in response to the life it lives. Another is that he can't bear to confront his own thickening body; he resents not having been able to freeze himself at the golden peak of his athletic stardom. A solution might be to tackle their weight problem (George's weight problem) together.

But the cruelty of George's rejection has cost Esther all that she once felt for him, and most of her own self-respect besides. She hurtles between extremes of self-hatred and self-pity; sometimes, in despair, she'll even seize a handful of her own flesh, as if she'd like to tear it off. George's contempt has filled her with such anger, there's no room left in her mind for a rational attitude toward her obesity; she no longer sees it as a problem with a solution, but only as a weapon against him.

Esther has sampled every "miracle" diet known: Atkins, Stillman, Scarsdale, Beverly Hills, Cambridge; safflower, grapefruit, vinegar. With all of them she's lost weight, and with all of them it's come right back, and then some. What never changes is her urge to turn to food for solace, and revenge. Baking a three-layer coconut cake while George is at the office and devouring the whole thing before he comes home, meeting him at the door with her mouth ringed with icing, not only gives some satisfaction to her unloved body, it's also Esther's only effective gesture of defiance.

Angela works at a television station, where eight years ago she met Frank when he came there as a sportswriter. Frank is a wiry, tense man, a lifelong chain smoker who managed to quit only when his father died of lung cancer; after five years, his fingers still occasionally twitch for a cigarette. Anxiety is his motor. His nerves are strung so tight he almost quivers; he looks as though if you touched him, he'd twang. He's got a mean streak a yard wide, and an incipient ulcer.

What keeps the ulcer from eating through is Angela, his wife, a buttery blonde with an easy laugh, a voice of honey, and soft, warm eyes. Angela's ripe, big-breasted body with its deep curves and candid belly has, to tell the truth, been around. Before Frank appeared, most of the guys had gone out with Angela at least a few times—whatever it took to get her into bed. But no more than that. She's great at home, in the dark, but in public they're ashamed of her. "Go out with that cow? Listen, I'm not that hard up—do I need to take a woman who looks like my mother out on dates?"

Angela's younger than any of them and she's not fat—the curves are firm—but she's a full-bodied woman. Their brutality betrays more than shame; it reflects a fear of the appeal of a woman like Angela: She's a challenge to their virility. They're intimidated by her, obscurely sensing that surrender to her might mean being overwhelmed by her.

Not Frank. To him, Angela is Venus—and Venus is no skimpy snippet. Angela is his horn of plenty, his wealth. He understands too well the depth of his need for her to give a damn what anybody else thinks. He's not afraid of being engulfed by her; all he's worried about is losing her. Frank knows his own capacities for sourness, for a shabby cynicism, a small, dry, pinched existence. Angela is his link to life; without her, he'd shrivel into a rasping husk.

Since their marriage Angela's beauty has taken on a new glow. She watches her weight, just as she always has, having known since she was a teenager that controlling it was going to demand lifelong attention. Gluttony and sloth will always be waiting to claim her. But she works at keeping active and supple, curbing her appetite, refusing to let her curves swell into obesity. And Frank's love and appreciation have given her a pride in her body that makes it easy.

Food: Venus in the Kitchen

How does Angela do it? She follows a few simple rules.

(1) She doesn't believe in sentencing herself—or Frank—to a life of Spartan self-denial. She makes all his favorite dishes, but serves herself half of what she gives him (he never gains weight). She eats everything, but in small portions.

(2) Her mainstay is the endo's greatest ally, the complex carbohydrates. The single most important weight control secret for endos is *volume*. Those big endo stomachs cry out to be filled up, and the foods that are highest in low-calorie volume are the carbohydrates. Composed largely of cellulose and fiber, they offer the most satisfaction for the fewest calories. Whole grains, vegetables, and fruits constitute 70 percent of Angela's diet.

She avoids concentrated calories, emphasizes bulk. Every night before dinner she fixes herself a plate of raw vegetables as an appetite spoiler. When she's hungry during the day she'll make a bowl of plain popcorn (two and a half cups are only 100 calories).

High-fiber, high-residue foods move more rapidly through the digestive system, so that fewer of their calories are absorbed. The high-fiber, high-carbohydrate diet also protects against digestive and intestinal disorders, including cancer of t colon, besides being low in fat, which is implicated in many degenerative diseases. But its main advantage for endos is the favorable ratio of volume to calories; carbohydrates are filling without being fattening.

(3) Angela weighs herself every morning. If she's gone two pounds over her ideal weight, she swings immediately into her automatic "juice routine," a day of low-calorie fluids: Every three hours she has a glass of vegetable or fruit juice freshly prepared in a blender. Pineapple-grapefruit-strawberry, watermelon-banana-apple, tomato-cucumber-green pepper, carrot-lettuce-parsley are favorite combinations.

More tips:

- Always divide your calories among a number of meals a day. Eating temporarily increases the metabolic rate, which means that several small meals burn calories more efficiently than one or two big ones.

- Because the "appestat" in the hypothalamus (the hunger center in the brain) is cued to temperature, hot foods— especially liquids—satisfy appetite faster than anything else. Next to carbohydrates, hot soups, bouillon, tea, and coffee are an endo's best friends. Begin every meal with a clear hot soup, eat it slowly to give your brain the chance to receive the sensation of satiety, and your hunger will quickly pass. If you get hungry at night, try a cup of hot bouillon.

- Iced drinks, such as iced tea and coffee, numb the palate temporarily; they can help reduce hunger between meals.

- Slightly acid foods cut "mouth hunger." Try eating a pickle or drinking a glass of grapefruit juice or buttermilk before and between meals (buttermilk, contrary to its name, has many fewer calories than whole milk; it's about the same as skim milk).

Exercise: Kinetic Curve Control

The best, the fastest, the most painless and permanent strategy for getting it off, keeping it off, *and* feeling good while you're doing it is to combine diet with exercise. In fact, calorie cutting alone rarely works for endos; overweight is far more often the result of inactivity than of overeating. Attacking the problem from both sides of the energy equation, increasing outgo as you reduce income, is much more likely to give you permanent success in weight control. And you'll find that the whole process feels less like deprivation, more like being good to yourself, with big bonuses in increased energy and well-being.

First, a piece of simple arithmetic: With daily exercise, you needn't cut back so drastically on your intake of food in order to lose the same amount of weight as you would with dieting alone. In one study, women who took a half-hour daily walk lost twenty-two pounds a year without dieting at all.

More important still, exercise—especially aerobic (continuous, heart-pumping) exercise—produces a "halo effect" that raises the rate at which your body burns calories for several hours after you've stopped exercising.

And embarking on a regular exercise program that gets your body moving for an hour a day in some form of aerobics (walking, swimming, jogging, bicycling) actually reduces hunger, and speeds up weight loss far beyond the caloric expenditure of the exercise alone.

You don't feel hungry immediately after exercising; many endos find their low-calorie lunch more satisfying if they take a brisk walk just before lunchtime. Far from "working up an appetite," exercise revs up your metabolism so that you're content with less food.

What's more, most endos report that within a week after embarking on a daily exercise routine, they no longer feel raging hunger pangs at *any* time. Those irresistible impulses to binge have also vanished. You'll feel generally more in control of your appetite—which exercise tends to stabilize or even reduce—and of your life. A number of recent studies have shown, too, that exercise alone compares very favorably with psychotherapy in the relief of depression.

Regular exercise will also put you in touch with your body as you may never have been before. You'll develop a new sensitivity to what's going on within, feel a new connectedness, an integration between inside and outside.

If you've been very sedentary or have more than twenty pounds to lose:

• Begin with walking. Start at twenty minutes a day; increase time and distance gradually. Work up to an hour; cover four miles. You'll probably have to push yourself at first; push gently but steadily. You're conditioning your body to a new and permanently higher level of activity. Don't rush the process, but don't give yourself excuses for skipping either.

- If you drive to work, an easy way to incorporate aerobic-
  conditioning walking into your life is to park your car a mile
  from your office and walk that mile twice a day. Gradually
  increase the distance at which you park the car to two miles.
  This will give you a half-hour's walk each way; doing it daily
  will give you excellent aerobic fitness.

You may feel at first that moving your body is more difficult
than the rigors of dieting—but this is all the more reason not
to surrender to inertia. You can mobilize a lot of stubborn
stick-to-itiveness when you want to, and once the habit is
established you'll find it easy to maintain.

Walking will probably be the most natural way of getting
more movement into your life to begin with, but the most
enjoyable, liberating exercise for endos is:

- Swimming. All endos are water babies; it's your element. In
  the water you shed the burden of your weight and find a
  new freedom; there, your bulk is an asset. Fat tissue weighs
  far less than muscle or bone, so that the higher the
  proportion of fat in your body, the more buoyant you are.

And swimming puts no strain at all on the weight-bearing
joints that often give you trouble. In fact, doctors often
recommend swimming as the ideal therapy for arthritis and
other joint disorders, and to help heal joint injuries. Swimming works all the muscles of the body too; it's great for
developing upper-body strength, which most other aerobics
don't do. It's sensuous, sociable, and relaxing. And, most
important if you're out of condition, the water's resistance
makes it almost impossible to overstress the heart; water
offers a built-in protection against overdoing without knowing it. (Needless to say, if you are seriously overweight, suffer
from high blood pressure, diabetes, or a heart condition, or
have any chronic health problem, it's imperative to get a
doctor's okay before you embark on *any* exercise program.)

Aerobic benefits from swimming begin when you can swim
at least twenty minutes without stopping. But what if your
heart will do it, but your muscles aren't strong enough?

• Follow a calisthenics program, using wrist and ankle weights to add more resistance. Or you can hold light dumbbells (two to five pounds) as you go through your workout. With either, you'll build greater strength, and build it faster, than if you use your body's resistance alone. For best results, spend twenty minutes to half an hour two or three times a week.

2. MESO ENDOS:
   Buoyant and Bubbly

Who You Are

Generosity, of body and of spirit, rules here. Your dominant endo, with meso at secondary strength, gives you a temperament of vibrant vitality, an effortless outpouring of expansive energy. Meso, the energy component, is lower than endo but it outweighs ecto, the component of inhibition and restraint. Your endo emotional warmth is infused with meso vigor and drive, and the brakes are off besides; you meso endos have formidably forceful personalities that are totally extraverted.

With you, everything is on the surface. You withhold nothing; whatever you are is fully displayed. You live to express yourselves, and you seldom look within. When you do, you like what you see there; you're not given to self-criticism. You're exuberantly confident and optimistic.

You like to live on a grand scale; you "think big." Your houses tend to be large but nonetheless crowded with objects proclaiming your status as the most conspicuous of consumers. You buy the giant size, by the dozen. Too much is never enough, and your taste inclines to turn-of-the-century opulence: gilded mirrors, ornate furniture, glistening chandeliers, heavy bronze candelabra—and soft, deep armchairs (comfort always takes precedence over grandeur). Your bedrooms are swathed in fur, plated with mirrors: "I like to see how I'm doing," explained meso endo Mae West, whose bedroom—walls and ceiling—was entirely mirror-lined. Even with the less extravagant among you, every surface tends to be either decorated or occupied.

In person, too, meso endos are seldom understated; you like vivid, boldly cut clothes that flaunt your robust curves. You take up a lot of psychic space, crowding every room you're in, radiating waves of emotional energy in all directions. You're noisy, showy, and vital, and you like to create a stir—"make a spectacle of themselves," say your ecto friends sourly—wherever you go. Your responses are simple and vociferous: "I hate it"; "I love her"; "Get him *out* of here!"

Your emotions are easily stirred; you're happiest in a state of emotional release. You're the people who sob unashamedly in the movies. What you most love is to be swept by a belly-deep gust of feeling, and your energy tends to go into the expression of feeling rather than in taking action or thought. You make the most rousing public speakers, orators, preachers, evangelists, and you're always your own best audience, moving yourself to tears with your throbbing sincerity. It's among you that most of the great voices are to be found: Caruso and Churchill, Orson Welles and Pavarotti, Flagstad, Nilsson, Callas.

All or Nothing

Meso endos have primary-colored minds. You like to keep things as clear and simple as possible, preferring to think in broad, comprehensive categories. You have little tolerance for ambiguity or contradictions, for shadows and subtleties; your instinct is to drag a complex or cloudy issue into the bright sunlight, so that you can come down heavily and strongly on one side, wholly excluding the other. A thing is either good or bad, true or false; you either reject it or embrace it totally.

This has nothing to do with intelligence; it's a trait of temperament that is found equally in the brightest and the most dim-witted among you. You want to feel and do everything "one hundred percent," the full force of your enthusiasm surging behind a social issue, a political candidate, a corporate decision. What you don't like is having to hold contradictory aspects of a situation suspended in your mind. More than anything else, you hate internal conflict; determined to keep your feelings intact, you insist on plumping down immediately on one side of what may be a multifaceted problem. "Stop making everything so damned complicated!" you cry when anyone tries to forestall a premature rush to judgment.

Comfort is always your goal, and a mind made up is a mind at ease. Inconsistency doesn't trouble you nearly as much as ambivalence. You'll change your mind—although reluctantly and only if you have to—to meet changing circumstances, but indecision or uncertainty are intolerable. You either decide immediately or push the entire issue under the carpet. And once you've chosen your side, you like to round the whole thing off in a reassuring formula: "Win a few, lose a few"; "My country, right or wrong."

You're good problem solvers, competent and realistic, and operating from a solid base of common sense. You make highly effective politicians of the hardheaded sort who specialize in finding solutions to concrete and clear-cut problems, and your ideas are always workable. Seldom are you seekers or probers to the hidden heart of things; you're not particularly interested in uncovering underlying laws or principles, nor do you often take the lead in deciding which policy to follow. But once the goal has been chosen, you're unbeatable at organizing the most efficient deployment of the available forces. Let the others tell you where they want to go, and you'll get them there. More often strategists than theoreticians, pragmatists than dreamers, you're the great experts in the art of the possible. You ask not "what?" or "why?" but "how?" And your firm grasp of the actual serves as a valuable corrective to meso flights of ego and ecto flights of fancy.

When you become leaders it's more often thanks to your ability to bring warring factions together and unite them at least temporarily in a common cause. But when you seek leadership, it's in order to be part of the action rather than to run things. You'll take charge because someone has to, in order to keep the game going, but you're indifferent to achieving authority for yourself, for its own sake. A meso who finds his access to power blocked for any reason will either change course, shift his alliances, or pull out. It's the leadership role he's after, not mere membership. But your loyalties go first to the group, and you find it easy to merge your personal ambition with the group's interests and welfare. You care less about power than a meso does, and more about belonging.

The Undivided Heart

What's most typical of you meso endos, at work or at play, is an enormous perseverance. When you get stuck or reach a dead end and can't bulldoze through, you just turn back and start all over again, with exactly the same implacable determination with which you started out. You have an elephantine patience that keeps going through every obstacle, without complaint, without yielding, without stopping.

Inertia means not only "a body at rest tends to remain at rest," but also "a body in motion tends to remain in motion," and that second sense is constantly being illuminated for anyone living with or working alongside you. Your critics say you lack the insight to know when you ought to stop, that it's nothing but blind momentum that carries you along, wrongheadedly as often as not.

But it's you who give heart to any difficult undertaking; you're the survivors who pull others through with you. It's your inner wholeness, your refusal to entertain doubts or negative thoughts, that gives you such indomitable courage. If you're sometimes unimaginative, you also lack the "imagination of disaster"—or defeat.

Like Harry, a butcher's son from Cracow, a thickset middle-aged man who is a street trader on Forty-seventh Street, New York's wholesale diamond district. Today he walks around with one pocket full of uncut diamonds and the other full of cash, but Leon, a colleague on the street, remembers him in Auschwitz. He was carrying twenty people "on his back" then (Leon was one of them), having charged himself with the responsibility of stealing enough food to keep them alive when they were too weak to fend for themselves; many times a day he risked his life without thought for anything but their need.

Meso endos are highly gregarious. Whether your community is a university, an army barracks, a corporate headquarters, a high school, a newspaper office, or the floor of the Senate, within that arena you seem to be everywhere at once. You're endowed by nature with an incessant, bustling social energy. But although you're with people virtually nonstop, your judgment of them is often poor. Your exuberant outgoingness tends to blunt your perceptions of others; you usually miss entirely those subtle, almost subliminal signals that play so large a part in our intuitive understanding of people. An amusing companion, fun to have drinks or dinner with, especially if he or she confirms your existing ideas and prejudices, is a "great guy," a "terrific gal"—and that's all you meso endos need to know; there's no reason to look deeper.

The comfortable haze of warmth and good fellowship in which you like to live at all times is not conducive to sensing differences among people, and in fact you tend to resist discrimination of every kind—which is one of your charms. But if there's any discrepancy between someone's surface and the reality beneath, you'll be the last to see it.

In one sense, everything is personal to you, but in another, nothing is. To you we're all pretty much alike. You're at your best when what's needed are the basics: food, shelter, love. But understanding, when it demands an act of imagination, a movement of empathy toward someone unlike yourself, is usually beyond you.

The paradox of outgoing, extraverted people is that in fact you don't move out toward others; you bring them toward yourself, reaching out and enfolding them in a loving embrace that pulls them into *your* orbit. A self-forgetfulness that can leap a psychological distance toward the other *in* his otherness, acknowledging and valuing it for its difference from you, is not at all your style. Understanding means preserving distinctions, and what you want is to merge. You'd always rather feel and experience than know. Even when depressed, you don't retreat away, inside yourself. It's an extraverted depression; you display your mood, with dramatic groans and a postural slump anybody can read a mile away.

"Life Is Sensation"

You have a bottomless appetite for stimulation, the brighter and louder the better. You're the most avid audiences for spectacle: musical comedy, opera, nightclubs, circuses, sporting events. Especially music, whose appeal is its direct pipeline to the emotions; music stirs the feelings more viscerally and immediately than any of the other arts. But you love every form of action, "thrills," that can be experienced vicariously, in comfort. Las Vegas and Atlantic City were created to satisfy your craving for low-risk excitement. Like Winston Churchill, you feel that "Life is sensation; sensation is life."

All your senses are strong, but you have a particularly uninhibited sense of smell. Many people prefer not to smell anything at all; even a delicate perfume is suspect, and anything stronger is "vulgar," even cooking smells, not to mention more earthy odors. But meso endos actively enjoy smells of all kinds, including garlic, pungent cheese, even sweat. Almost any odor at all that's a sign of life, not excepting strong animal smells, is a positive pleasure.

You have a particularly intense need for "stroking," for gestures of recognition and affection. It's never enough for you to hear, once, that you are loved. Ectos feel that one such statement should suffice for all time, because when an ecto says "I love you," it's written on the stars. Repetition would be redundant. But you need both to say it and to hear it as often as possible—not because you're less sincere or it's less deeply felt, but because to you the expression of feeling is its whole reality. Love doesn't exist unless and until it's being demonstrated.

You have a practically continuous need for caressing and hugging. You'll seize any excuse to make physical contact, turning even a social kiss in a theater lobby or a restaurant into a smothering bear hug and a shower of wet smacks (where an ecto will lean forward on tiptoe for a dry, tentative little peck).

These differences are inherent in your body structure. Where ectos—biologically overexposed, with an excess of skin surface relative to their total body mass—are wary of stimulus, meso endos (biologically underexposed, with more mass than surface) are greedy for it. You love every form of stimulus—sound, light, taste, smell—but your craving for touch is strongest of all. You can never get enough skin contact—not because your skin is so sensitive, but just because it isn't.

Your skin is soft, plump, and satiny, thanks to its generous layer of subcutaneous fat. But fat tissue is poorly supplied with blood vessels and nerve endings, which makes it relatively inert and unresponsive. The more inviting the skin, the less sensitive it is, and the more stimulation it needs in order to feel anything.

This "stimulus hunger" is acute in everyone in the early years; it's well known that babies need physical stroking merely to stay alive. In adults, the need for direct physical contact can be satisfied to some extent by "recognition stroking," nonphysical gestures of appreciation: "Gee, you're terrific! What would I do without you?" "I've never heard that aria sung so beautifully." "Nobody can set a table like Rosalie."

Your threshold of arousal is high. Stimuli must be frequent and strong before you can experience them. And internal sensations are always the weakest; it's stimulation of the surface to which you most readily respond. Both the men and women among you need much more hugging and kissing and caressing than sexual intercourse itself; sex is not an isolated impulse, but one sensual pleasure among many others, and not even necessarily at the top of the list. Sex for you is an item on a continuum that includes drinking and chatting, music and jokes, even arguments and fights, not to mention food. In the final analysis, sex is what comes after dinner.

Your energy is normally both high and lasting. The usual office schedule of an eight- or nine-hour working day with an hour's break for lunch is a waste of your vitality. When you're able to set up your own schedule, you can accomplish far more. What you usually prefer is five or six hours of uninterrupted concentration on the task at hand. Then you like to rest for a couple of hours, taking a complete break (this can mean bath, pajamas, and bed). After that you're good for another five or six hours at the same high level as before.

"I Feel Very Lonely Without a War"

This century's most renowned meso endo, who exhibited all the traits in the most colorful manner imaginable, was Winston Churchill. Churchill was unusual in being one of the very few men ever to rise to a position of national political leadership who was not a predominant meso. It was this dominant endo that infused his personality with zest, warmth, and an almost theatrical sense of history and of his own place in it.

Churchill spoke for all meso endos when he said—as he frequently did—"All my life I have paid more attention to self-expression than to self-discipline." All his life, too, he suffered from his famous "Black Dog," a periodic depression apparently inherited from his Marlborough ancestors, but it was always short-lived, quickly thrown off by the reassertion of his temperamental optimism and gusto. "We are all worms," he told a friend as a young man, "but I do believe that I am a glow-worm."

It was in part Churchill's dramatic vision of the role Britain was to play in the war that enabled him to rally Parliament and the people in 1940. No one who was alive then will forget how in that darkest hour, when England was facing, it seemed, certain and imminent invasion, a gruff voice, buoyed by a ferocious, stubborn gaiety, heartened and fortified them against dread. Churchill's meso endo voice, which he used to great and conscious effect, was a crucial element in his political success. The voice—even more than the cigar, the pugnacious, obstinate bulldog face, or the resolute set of his sturdy body—is what people remember from that breathless summer, the voice from the radio that alone opposed the terrifying force of Hitler's demonic raving.

Churchill's ebullience, his delight in his own powers, was

infectious. Harold Nicolson wrote of him in the House of Commons: "He finds it difficult to conceal his enjoyment of his speech, and that, in fact, is part of his amazing charm. He thrusts both his hands deep into his trouser pockets, and turns his tummy now to the right, now to the left, in evident enjoyment of his mastery of the position."

When Churchill came to power in 1939 he was sixty-five—retirement age. Nevertheless, when the war was over he felt dejected. "I've had five years of continuous excitement. . . . I feel very lonely without a war." When Lady Macmillan asked him, "Which year of all your life, if you could relive one twelvemonth, would you choose?" Churchill replied, "Nineteen-forty, every time, every time!"

Blurred Boundaries

Your rejection of negativity extends to your own feelings as well. Vindictiveness, envy, and spite are all alien to your nature. You make bad haters. A broad and generous tolerance characterizes all of your dealings with others, and in old age you will attribute your longevity not to moderate habits or good genes but to a lifelong refusal to bear a grudge or let the sun go down on a quarrel.

You're always the last to believe evil of anyone; if you're compelled to, you're always astonished—not that people can be corrupt or wicked, but that the corruption not *show*. Never secretive or two-faced yourselves, you're not alert to these tendencies in anyone else. If your friend or partner has been caught falsifying the data, taking bribes, or selling secrets to the enemy, you're at first utterly disbelieving: "Roy? It's not possible! Why, I've known him since we were boys!" (Or, "But we were army buddies!" Or, "He was my roommate in law school!") In other words, the externals were all in order.

You'll stubbornly defend your friend as long as possible. If the evidence against him is persuasive, however, you'll suffer agonies but yield to the facts—the revised externals. And once you're convinced that someone you loved and trusted has betrayed that trust, you'll cast him off completely, and do without hesitation whatever has to be done: fire him, testify against him, pass a sentence of execution. What you never do is prolong the agony or choose the individual over the institution. If a choice must be made, your allegiance will always go to the club, the corps, the firm. Honor and the code of the tribe always take precedence over personal loyalties.

When that chapter is closed, you'll never think of the matter again. You resolutely refuse to dwell on past griefs. You make a clean break, then bandage the wound with a summing-up epithet: "He was a traitor." "A wrong 'un." "She lied." Period, end of sentence. No questioning or searching into whys or wherefores. The door slams shut, and life goes on.

Your loyalty to and identification with the group tend to blur your sense of boundaries. Distinctions between self and other, me and you are fluid. To you it's "us," all flowing along together on the Great Stream of Life. You can be capable of an astonishing "selflessness," for your own sense of self, your personal ego, is not hedged around with any sharp feeling of separateness. Your generosity is literally boundless, because the difference between giving and receiving is so unimportant—you're as openhanded as you are greedy.

Living with the Life Force

You're usually happiest with people not very different from yourself. You flamboyant meso endo women are forever falling for gentle, soft-spoken men, drawn to an elusive melancholy that seems to promise romantic intensity. This rarely materializes, and such attachments seldom last. You're too exhausting for this type of man to live with for long. (One of them sighed, when asked where he was going for his vacation: "Wherever Anita doesn't. Just getting away from her for a week is all the vacation I need.") And the men aren't zesty or gutsy enough for you.

You meso endo men, too, are drawn to quiet, self-effacing types as friends and lovers, people who don't mind letting you have all the limelight, who are willing to serve as a permanent, portable audience. You demand a lot of reassurance and support, since you're always on the verge of "going too far"; you need to be told you're still loved even after committing outrageous excesses. Whenever you're criticized for any of your doings, you run and relay it to your cronies, demanding to hear the hard words contradicted. You like to have people around you who will defend you in everything you do.

But what you *need* is someone as stubborn as you are who can make you see reason when you're in the wrong. What you'll often do is seek out such people, install them in this role of critic, then ever after tirelessly complain what a drag they are. That's the relationship—and a surprisingly solid and enduring one it frequently turns out to be. You need to make a display of resisting these counselors loudly and fiercely, while knowing very well you'd be headed for disaster without them. Although it sometimes happens, too, that having a manager, a wife, or a husband to act as a monitor actually encourages you to behave more extravagantly than ever.

Like Harvey, who made millions in the cement business. Harvey is an inveterate joiner, the mainstay of his many clubs and the life force behind every class reunion. After a few drinks Harvey is likely to get into a boozily sentimental chat with an old fraternity brother, who by sheerest chance turns out to be chairman of the alumni building committee. More than once a hung-over Harvey has been rudely reminded the next morning by an excited phone call from the president that in his alcoholic glow he promised to build the university a new computer center or football stadium. What a relief to be able to pass the phone silently across the breakfast table to Charlotte, his wife and official spoilsport. Charlotte does the explaining, the apologizing, the soothing of disappointed hopes—and somehow also bears the burden of any lingering bad feeling. Charlotte's the household heavy, while ever-lovable Harvey goes galloping on, a big-hearted pushover for any worthy cause.

Your sympathies are easily aroused, and you're famously openhanded, even though your most dramatic gestures of generosity may be withdrawn the next day, like Harvey's. You have a way of turning deaf and distant to any expectation, however just or urgent; you'll pull back from the least hint of a demand or an assumed obligation. You'll give lavishly, but only from an overflowing heart; you have to feel that the impulse originated with you.

You're especially susceptible to any project intended to

break down barriers or bridge distances between people. You're the ones who are always saying, "I know that if we could just sit down and really *talk* to the Russians, they'd see that we're all pretty much alike at heart; we really want the same things." It's instinctive with you to feel that all divisions, all fences are unnatural and bad. You always brighten when anyone suggests building "world friendship centers" or sending up balloons to circle the planet bearing messages of good will and hope to the "family of man."

Hollywood's Wife of Bath

One exorbitant meso endo personality who is coming into her richest bloom only now, as she advances into her fifties, is Elizabeth Taylor. The innate vitality and vulgarity that were suppressed when she was merely an enameled MGM object, "the most beautiful woman in the world," have burst forth as she's come into her florid prime, and now she's like some elemental force of nature. She's become a lovable bawd, our own Wife of Bath, a shamelessly rowdy beauty, and she's given a shot in the arm to the morale of meso endo women everywhere.

When Hedda Hopper scolded her for her blazingly public affair with the married Eddie Fisher, whom she snatched away from Debbie Reynolds soon after Mike Todd was killed, she retorted, "Mike's dead and I'm alive. What do you expect me to do, sleep alone?" It took years for the public to forgive her, but she didn't mean it heartlessly; it was just that for meso endos only the present exists. Now is so bright, so alive, so responsive to cries of "I want! I want!" that neither past nor future nor any gray inhibiting considerations of "good taste" or self-restraint can possibly compete.

Taylor lives not so much like royalty—what modern royalty could afford it?—as like some outlandish barbarian queen, striding the globe and howling for tribute, good-natured but meaning it. She's all appetite, famous for having chili and pastrami sandwiches flown in from Beverly Hills to London or Rome or wherever her caravan has encamped. To see a bracelet of shiny stones or an opulent fur is to shriek, "Gimme that!" But although each of the string of husbands has covered her with jewels, none of them ever succeeded in subduing her into a status object or an accessory to his own career. She's flung every one of them behind her without breaking stride in her triumphant onward march.

For most of her life Elizabeth Taylor Hilton Wilding Todd Fisher Burton Burton Warner has been a staple of gossip columnists all over the world. By this time it's hard to imagine what scandal she could stir up, or what an "exposé" of her doings would consist of; she's all exposure to begin with. What secrets could she possibly be harboring? Everything she has and is, she offers up for all the world to marvel at.

Well-being for Meso Endos

Rendezvous with Yourself

Resisting as you do any deferment of pleasure, sensual or emotional, you're always too impetuous, too greedy to experience (devour, really) whatever is offered—sometimes even before it's offered. Learn to wait, to refrain from hurling yourself instantly upon everything that looks good. You tend to overwhelm whatever attracts you, and often, if it's a person, he or she will instinctively recoil, staggering under the assault and pulling away from you.

Savor more slowly; let the object, the person, the moment unfold itself to you; learn to receive without grabbing. You don't have to rush at an experience in order to possess it. Rather than flooding every moment with feeling, learn to hold back a little in the expression of your emotions. Cultivate the ability to be passive and attentive at the same time—which doesn't come naturally; to you, being quiet means being asleep. But if you can learn to be both alert and still, converting some of your outgoing vitality into receptiveness; if you can sometimes wait, watch, and listen with the same energy with which you express yourself, you'll be rewarded by an immediate enriching of your experience of the sensual world that is your element and your delight.

Because there *is* a world out there, separate from you, and unless you can acknowledge its independent existence you're likely to be hurt and bewildered by its rejection of you—not to mention that any life that is only self-referring, knows only itself, is a prison. Let your generosity expand to include, paradoxically, inhibition—the inhibition of your overflowing, overwhelming warmth. You're not the only sun in the world, although you often act as if you were. Your most urgent need is for love; then give lesser lights, fainter voices, a chance to shine and be heard. They'll love you infinitely more if you don't always blot them out with your radiance.

• Try this experiment: Write down everything you can remember about the appearance and characteristic behavior of someone you know well. Include as many details as possible about him or her, from head to foot: how he dresses, moves, speaks, his attitudes, his preferences, his whole mode of being. You'll probably be embarrassed to discover that all you can summon up at first is a blur; that all you're really aware of is your feelings about him.

But persevere. Look intently at the picture in your mind. Like a photograph in a developing bath, more and more details about the person will come crowding back to you if you just sit still and look inward—details you didn't remember noticing. And how vivid and distinctive the picture becomes, compared with its initial vagueness. You'll begin to realize how much of your life is lost to you in your blunted perceptions, generalized feelings.

• Practice your powers of observation. Look closely at the details in the objects or people you see before you; register them consciously. Then try drawing them, or describing them in words. The attempt itself to render a person or thing, to give form to it, will bring it alive in your mind. And how its being eludes your pencil! How complex and unique each thing is! If you practice, you'll be surprised at the sharpness and precision your senses can develop, the refinement—and the enhanced pleasure they can give you. Your greatest challenge is to develop the capacity to stand back, to look and listen, to observe, without needing to take charge; to receive without reacting.

• Develop the capacity to be alone. If you can't stand being alone, you're too often forced into situations and company you'd never choose if you weren't in continual need of emotional supplies from outside yourself. *Practice* being alone, and still. If it makes you feel panicky or empty, try meditating in a room by yourself. A good technique for you is to sit quietly, in any position that's comfortable, and simply follow the movement of your breath in and out of your body. That's all; don't interfere with it, change it, or control it—just watch it. Do this for fifteen minutes at first, work up to an hour. This gives you a new kind of experience, of getting in touch with your inner self—which, like the other lesser voices, is usually drowned out by the trumpets of your overriding extraverted social self.

Food: Curbing the Curves

You meso endos have sturdy skeletons that can accommodate all the fat your endo component can lay on them, over the solid underpinning of muscle contributed by your meso. And you're high-energy people, given to excess in all directions, perhaps most of all in eating. Which adds up to the greatest potential for weight gain of any group. Not that you have to be fat—but you do need to take active steps to avoid it, and avoiding it is essential for both your health and your looks.

• Follow the dieting tips for balanced endos on pages 51–52. In addition, you should:

• Cut back sharply on your intake of fat—both animal and vegetable—and increase your intake of high-fiber foods such as raw fruits and vegetables (with the skin on, if it's edible). There's almost always an inverse ratio between the proportion of fat and of fiber you consume, and a high-fiber, low-fat diet helps prevent many diseases. Your present diet probably consists of from 35 to 40 percent fat; aim at 20 percent.

• Get most of your protein from vegetable sources. As a group, you're at the second-highest risk for cardiovascular disease (heart attacks and strokes). Animal protein increases blood cholesterol, an important risk factor in cardiovascular disease, while vegetable proteins lower it. They're much lower in calories by volume, too, comfortably filling your capacious stomachs while helping you shed pounds.

• Vegetable proteins supply all the essential amino acids of complete (animal) protein when eaten in the following combinations:

Rice	with	wheat legumes sesame seeds
Wheat	with	legumes soybeans and peanuts soybeans and sesame seeds rice and soybeans
Legumes	with	corn, rice, wheat, sesame seeds, barley, or oats

(Legumes include soybeans, peanuts, black-eyed peas, kidney beans, chickpeas, navy beans, pinto beans, and lima beans.)

Now you can see the nutritional logic behind those classic combinations of baked beans and brown bread, or red beans and rice.

• Learn to taste your food, to savor it, rather than wolfing it down. Experiment with seasonings; your "mouth hunger" can best be satisfied with spicy foods. The peppery Szechuan, Mexican, and Indian cuisines are high in vegetables, low in fat, strong on flavor.

Exercise: Shaping the Curves

Any weight-loss program for meso endos must attack the problem on two fronts: cutting back on calories while gradually but persistently increasing activity. You may have become physically lazy, but you've got plenty of willpower to call upon when you want to. Your problem is never lack of stamina, but mobilizing the will to get moving. As George Sheehan observes, it's not the flesh that's weak, but the spirit; the flesh is longing for a workout, which the indolent spirit denies it. But it's a good idea, especially if you've been sedentary for any length of time or have a lot of weight to lose, to get a thorough medical checkup before embarking on any exercise program.

• Start with a moderate regime of walking and swimming on alternate days; if you don't have access to a pool, walk every day. What you want are activities that demand a steady, even output of energy at a higher level than you use in your daily life. Don't begin with sports that demand high-intensity spurts of peak energy—they'll only exhaust you while contributing nothing to your fitness or to weight loss. You'll find you resist doing them, and feel spent afterward when you do. The point is not to knock yourself out once a week, but to condition yourself *gradually* to activity you can sustain without excessive fatigue for half an hour. If at first you're only good for fifteen minutes at a time, or even five, then do that—but keep at it, and keep returning to it. Increase time and distance gradually. You don't have to feel pain to get the benefits. Stay within your comfort zone—but be persistent. Work up to an hour a day alternately walking and swimming, or walking only. This will also increase your metabolism so that your body becomes a more efficient calorie-burning machine.

• Many of you have never called upon your meso potential for strength and shapeliness; you've left it lying inert beneath a blanket of endo fat. Don't let that potential go to waste. Working out with weights can radically alter your outline from flabby to firm, with beautifully defined contours. Follow the program outlined on pages 126–128.

• You tend to be bottom-heavy, with your weight concentrated around your stomach, hips, and thighs. A stationary bicycle will trim this area, and also confer aerobic benefits; it's even better than actual bicycles, which today are built so efficiently that they don't demand enough effort to constitute useful aerobics.

• As you work on trimming your lower body with the weight-training plan and aerobics, you can balance your proportions by developing your upper body. Two excellent machines: The Bullworker, an inexpensive portable machine available in health stores, is a simple spring resistance device that develops shoulders, arms, back, and chest. And a rowing machine, while much more expensive, gives an excellent aerobics workout, with the advantage for meso endos that it not only develops the upper body, which most aerobics don't do, but also firms and shapes the thighs.

3. ECTO ENDOS:
Soft and Sinuous

Who You Are

You're the shy exhibitionists. In you ecto endos, not only is meso, the component of energy and assertive action, the lowest of the three, but your two dominant components, endo and ecto, are often in conflict. You're complex and contradictory people, a mystery to others and sometimes to yourselves. You're creatures of mirrors and masks.

Because you want both to reveal and to conceal yourself, to shine and to hide, you often resort to complicated role-playing: "Look at me! (But this isn't the *real* me.)" We all play a variety of social roles, but you seem to switch not only roles but selves so frequently, so smoothly, and with so little sense of inconsistency, you're like quick-change artists of the psyche. Actually it's all a strategy; by your speed and capriciousness in the manipulation of your many masks, you can catch the rest of us off balance.

But shyness versus showing off is only one of ecto endos' many contradictions. You can be equally—and simultaneously—warm and selfish, sociable and remote, dreamy and calculating, lonely and dependent, insecure and destructive. You seek out powerful people who can protect you, then insidiously try to undermine their strength. You can be submissive, self-effacing, and suspicious, all at once. You spend enormous energy keeping others guessing as to who or what you "really" are, but your own life is often an anxious quest for identity.

The key to much of your behavior, as is the case with everyone who is low in meso, is insecurity. When assertiveness and stamina are low, the capacity for self-affirming action is also low. More than most people, you're dependent upon others' response to you. You have a deep need to please, to intrigue, to amuse, not to offend. Too often you stake everything on your ability to seduce.

Ecto endo problems arise when you've handed control of your life over to someone else. It's tempting to let some stronger will take charge. But when your identity depends upon the image of yourself that you perceive in the gaze of others, the risks are only too obvious: If those others stop looking, you may stop existing. This is why you so often feel slightly unreal, as though you're giving a performance; you can't risk exposing your true self when it seems so vulnerable. Many of you feel that your best chance for survival lies in awakening the desire and protective instinct of another. Sometimes you're right, but too often it doesn't work out quite the way you had in mind.

You're intensely sensual, with a strong sex drive, but you

rarely yield to it; often you don't let yourself even admit to it. This is the one area in which you try to control instead of being controlled: You use your erotic imagination seductively, weaving an irresistible sensuous spell with a deftness that's almost instinctive.

Beginning with your surroundings. Many of you possess an uncommon flair for decorating, a sure sense of how to make the cleverest use of color, texture, space, and light to create surroundings that are both luxurious and relaxing, stimulating and soothing—an entrancing pleasure dome.

You're especially fond of shimmering surfaces and fabrics, soft and luminous: the sheen of satin; the ripple of watered silk; smoky mirrors; flowers floating in pools of water; pearly, opalescent glass; translucent curtains. You need flowers almost more than food. The colors you prefer are so pale as to be almost imperceptible, reflections upon water in sunshine: white, creamy or iced with blue; the green of a leaf's shadow; the yellow of sunlight; the palest blush of pink. You know a trick of illuminating your rooms with a pink so subtle it sheds no color but makes the skin glow, so that everyone around you looks and feels beautiful, relaxed, and happy.

Flashes and Fragments

You're intuitive rather than rational, attuned less to the external facts of a situation than to what isn't quite visible. You'll often seem numb or indifferent to what's going on around you, but you have an acute sensitivity to mood, picking up the emotional undercurrents in any encounter or gathering with uncanny quickness, responding to subliminal cues rather than the exterior reality. You yourselves are moody, too, mysterious and unpredictable, shifting in response to inner impulses unsensed by the people around you.

Your mind works primarily by association—not logical associations but emotional ones. Some person or thing stirs a memory or evokes an image of something else, which resembles the first only in the way you feel about them both. Since your frame of reference is entirely private, these associations are meaningless to anyone else, and therefore incommunicable; you often have trouble expressing yourself verbally, are liable to be misunderstood by those who take you literally.

Adding to the confusion is the suddenness with which the ecto endo mind moves—in what seem like wildly erratic, random leaps that nevertheless have a strange way of landing dead on target. You think not only intuitively but almost will-lessly, letting an image flower spontaneously in your mind without thought for where it came from or what it means. But you often have difficulty concentrating, and you're rarely able to carry out an extended train of thought or chain of rea-soning. Logic doesn't interest you—nor does consistency, nor seeing things whole. You tend to perceive isolated moments, separate bits, and can often miss something essential by failing to grasp the overall picture.

You're so startlingly illogical, sometimes, that to others you may seem dim-witted, but you have a way of hitting on truths inaccessible to more rational people. This is what we mean when we speak of someone who can "sniff out" the meaning or clue to a thing; it's an almost subconscious sense you have, like an animal's, inexplicable but often weirdly accurate, especially about latent possibilities. You can sometimes pre-dict the future, "smell" death coming, or danger, or victory. It's not extrasensory perception; your perceptions are wholly sensory, but you've absorbed them at a subliminal level of the self with which more practical people have lost touch.

As artists or makers of anything, you tend to produce fragments rather than completed works. Often you possess unusual artistic or literary talent, but as actors you have brilliant moments that you can't sustain throughout a per-formance; as writers you create marvelous individual images and scenes, but can't construct a strong narrative or story line; as painters your color sense is superb, your composition weak.

You're gifted impressionists, but poor mechanics and car-penters. What's most damaging, however, is your unwilling-ness to see how necessary these humbler skills are in creating anything durable. You feel, often rightly, that you're not receiving the recognition your talents deserve, but you lay the blame on the wrong doorstep. It isn't the insensitive public or neglectful and incompetent directors, editors, or gallery owners who have failed you; it's you yourselves who make poor custodians of your own gifts, demanding immediate success, instant stardom, while disdaining the role of patience and perseverance in any creative work.

And while you're anxiously seeking admiration and applause, at the same time you're curiously unable to take yourself and your talents seriously. Your hunger for achievement is fierce but intermittent; you work in fits and starts, brief spasms of frenetic energy that you can't maintain and that leave you limp and drained. It's as though steady but slow progress isn't dramatic and exciting enough; you need to whip yourself up by manufacturing crises and deadlines, then collapsing after each one.

And people who recognize your potential and want to help you realize it become exasperated with a frivolity that, after the brightest of beginnings, dissipates all your good intentions, so that finally, when the chips are down, you fail to deliver. You fall ill just before the previews; you leave the revisions and the "final polish" of the manuscript to the editor; the canvases remain sketches.

Psychic Striptease

In your quivering insecurity, you like to live swathed in mystery, concealed in veils and shadows, teasing and provoking, dropping hints suggesting that something, perhaps the central thing, is being held in reserve. Elusiveness is a potent element of your charm, until others realize that its purpose is to prevent them from seeing how few and feeble your resources really are. What terrifies you is the prospect that if you were ever to show your hand, to reveal yourself, the response would be: "Is that all?"

But when you're not besieged by anxiety, you ecto endos are the most delightful companions imaginable: playful, gentle, witty, sensitive, compliant. You know how to be both entertaining and the most appreciative of audiences. As a friend remarked, "Of course Jonathan is not the sort of person you can call up at three o'clock in the morning from the police station—but how often do you need to do that? And it's

unfortunately true that the people you can count on at three
A.M. are not always a hell of a lot of fun to be with the rest of
the time."

Your greatest liability is the fitful fluctuation of your
willpower. Either you can't make up your mind to act at all, or
you can act only on the spur of the moment: "If I don't do it
this second, I'll never do it." But those sudden urges
somehow are never about cleaning up the mess the morning
after or straightening out the chaos of your finances, but about
marrying someone you met yesterday or paying $8,000 you
don't have yet for an evening gown you've got to have now.

But you resist being pushed. Your impulses have to come
from within; they have to be yours, and you dig in your heels
when people try to pressure you. You're also easily depressed
and inclined to melancholy, as is true of most passive people.
You're capable of the most blinkered selfishness, but there's
something poignant and touching about you, too—and something stoical. Not taking yourself seriously includes your own
unhappiness and pain; like Ophelia or Cordelia, those gentle
victims, you seldom complain: "It's only me, after all." And
usually there are witnesses; you may suffer in silence, but
rarely alone.

For, like all endos, you have an instinct for friendship.
There's almost no limit to the burden you'll ask a friendship to
bear, and many of them buckle under the weight of your
needs and demands. But better than anyone else, you know
how to reel in a friend—just as he's about to cast off from you
for good—with such disarming humility, such sweetness in
your pleading, that the most disillusioned and obdurate heart
can only melt. "Please don't give up on me—oh, *please*! Don't
abandon me! Can't you see I'm doing my best? Don't turn
away! *Help me*!"

The Image of Desire

The heraldic emblem of your tribe should be a telephone,
rampant. "Keep in touch!" you cry each time you part from a
friend. "We'll talk soon!" And that's one promise you always
keep. The communications network you weave with a telephone is as tough and resilient as the transatlantic cable, and

reaches farther. You need frequent stretches of time alone—
solitude is your great restorative—but it's equally vital that
while physically alone you can feel connected with every
member of your far-flung community.

Some friends you speak with daily, others only every few
weeks, but you touch base with everyone in your world often
enough to keep the emotional connection alive. Some instinct
like a flower's or an insect's, buried but unerring, tells you
when "it's time" to check in with Nora or Evelyn or Herbert.
And some other sixth sense—or so you claim—tells you when
an unanswered ring on the other end is a sign of trouble.

Martha hasn't spoken to Lisa in several months, yet when
she does call and there's no answer, she's uneasy.

"I think something's wrong."

"Maybe she went away for a few days; after all, you haven't
talked to her since Christmas."

"That's true, but I still think there's something the matter. I
just have a feeling. I'm going to call John and ask him to drive
over and see."

Of course John discovers that Lisa has been in bed with
pneumonia for four days, too weak to stand up, drifting in
and out of consciousness with a high fever. Martha will only
say smugly, "It's just that I can always tell when a phone is
ringing in an empty room, and when it isn't. I knew she was
there."

Although—or because—you're so dependent, you find all
relationships difficult. Friendship, vital though it is, nevertheless demands from the friend a large tolerance for puzzling
or alarming behavior, and a willingness to give far more in the
way of patience and understanding than he or she will ever
get in return. The members of your social circle spend an
inordinate amount of time, it seems to them, trying to
interpret your actions. "When Susan and I got home that
night after the party, we lay in bed with our headaches asking
each other, 'Just what in *hell* did she think she was doing?
What sort of *statement* was she trying to make, running
around the terrace bare-assed playing the saxophone for
Jesus, for Christ's sake? . . . Not that Sasha ever needs an
excuse to shuck. . . . And then what was that business with

your earrings, when she grabbed them off you and put them on and told everybody they were all she was ever going to wear again in her whole life?' 'Well, they *were* a little loud. . . .'"

You uphold the aristocratic adage "Never apologize; never explain." You don't see that you have anything to apologize for, and you could never explain yourself anyway.

The fragmentation characteristic of the things you produce shows up in your behavior as well. You often seem unintegrated, as if you have trouble bringing yourself into focus—or rather, it's others who have the trouble; you're not particularly bothered by your own inconsistencies. You feel neither the urge nor the possibility of organizing your contradictory selves into some kind of unity. You simply exhibit those selves, one after the other, as the mood strikes you. One day it's the wonder-struck child; yesterday we got the femme fatale, and tomorrow it may be the tender earth mother, or perhaps the man-eating tigress. Whichever facet of yourself you choose to display, you play that role to the hilt, as though no other existed. Any confusion other people may feel is their problem.

To certain men, this quicksilver changeability is bewitching. The pursuit and capture of such an elusive tantalizer becomes for them a kind of obsession, in which more seems to be at stake than just another romance; perhaps it's the excitement of the hunt, with a human prey. Whatever the motive, trapping and pinning this butterfly to the wall absorbs all their energies, until they've got her. Then, of course, they have no idea what to do with her.

Others may be enslaved by your uncanny ability to incarnate the fantasy image of their desire, the girl of their most secret dreams, so that when they meet you, it's almost as if the longing had of itself brought you to life. And in a sense this is what has happened, for you have a mysterious way of seeming to become just what others want you to be. And you yourself achieve an identity, and a certain fulfillment, through impersonating a man's vision, becoming his *anima*, as Jung called it: the female shadow, or moon, side of the male psyche.

A flesh-and-blood woman who embodies a man's anima has a unique power over him, since she is actually a projection of his own unconscious. Ecto endo women often possess this power without understanding it or having any control over it—it's a power that the man confers upon you, rather than one you feel emanating from you. So you'll exploit it, but without having any real confidence in it.

What you yourself want is so hard to find, you'll sometimes spend your life drifting from one liaison to another in the search for it. You need a man who will take care of you without suffocating or crushing or boring you. Your problem is that few men who can offer you security can also touch you deeply enough for love; you need a rare combination of sensitivity and strength. You're the princess carried off by the knight in shining armor—one of the butterfly hunters, probably—to his castle, where you feel like a prisoner. And can only wait for another prince to come along and rescue you from the first.

The Twin Pillars

No amount of sad or frightening experience is likely to discourage you for long from seeking your salvation in love. No matter what else you have in your life, you'll always feel that your center of gravity, your compass north, is the man or woman in it. But basing the whole meaning of one's life on that one connection almost guarantees disaster. If love and work are the two great pillars that support the arc of self-esteem, you're too often tempted to build a leaning tower out of love alone—at the price, in the end, of finding yourself with neither.

Introspection through analytic therapy is usually not the answer. An ecto endo who looks inside sees only a void, and before long, if you get into the habit of peering within, the void will look increasingly like a vortex sucking you in. Too soon, you'll be trying to blot out consciousness of the void with alcohol and drugs, those perennial pitfalls of the passive.

What you need above all is the experience of success in acting on your own behalf, courageously committing yourself to a career, a project, or even a single task. The self-confidence

that comes from carrying any enterprise through to completion, creating something with a life of its own outside
yourself, is the surest cure for that feeling of sinking dread
that's one of your most constant companions.

Any decision to assume responsibility for your future has
an immediate brightening and bracing effect in the present,
just as surrender to passivity degenerates into a downward
spiral that will drown you in waves of helplessness and
hopelessness. And taking charge of your own life will also
sweeten all your dealings with others. Extreme dependence
goes hand in hand with mistrust; if you've given so much
power to others, how can you love them freely?

You've got a lively, fertile imagination that bubbles over
with plans and schemes, most of which never get past the
talking stage. The landscape of your life is strewn with the
bodies of your brainchildren, half-finished or barely begun:
projects and designs that were abandoned as soon as you ran
into difficulties. Just because ideas come to you so cheaply and
easily, you're always ready to drop any of them and flutter on
to the new one shining up ahead.

If you're fortunate, you'll have a partner or collaborator or
an institutional structure that compels you to see a piece of
work through to the end. And your collaborators are lucky,
too, to have you; quirky and complicated though you may be,
your talents are rare and indispensable. You're the people
who can make predictions based on intuition, and hit the
mark. You're the ones with the hunches as to which stocks are
likely to go up; whether the closing scene of the second act
will "play" as intended; which painter has something big in
him he hasn't yet got on canvas; from which area of scientific
or medical research the answer to a problem is going to come;
which obscure local politician will become the next national
figure; whether the book will sell, the movie will make it, the
TV show will find an audience. You've a flair for "sleepers,"
from frozen foods to pop records; in any array of possibilities
you can sense which one to back.

Subversive Whispers

These intuitions, of course, depend upon a long steeping in the subject; they don't come to you by magic. But you rarely can articulate the reasons for your choices. At first your collaborators ask, understandably, how you arrived at them. They soon learn better. The business partner of a gifted ecto endo says, "Frankly, I don't even want to know anymore why he chooses this one and not that one. I used to ask him to explain, but I soon learned to keep my mouth shut, just take what he said and be thankful. Otherwise I'd get something like, 'Well, I'd go with X because her mother was an ocean person and her father was a mountain person. . . .' No, it's better not to know."

One field for which you have a special gift is communications—not so much the content as the web of connections. You know how to keep the network from fraying, how to maintain it as a living organism so that even the most distant members feel linked directly to the heart. It was a small, whispery-voiced ecto endo woman who devised the system by which an international corporation was able to keep all of its clients stroked and happy throughout the turmoil of executive upheaval at the top that nearly tore the organization apart. Thanks to her, only the battling parties knew there was any trouble.

And you often possess a mysterious knack for keeping a stable of mettlesome egotists soothed and content. You make wonderful managers and midwives for every kind of artist, recognizing originality in others and knowing how to encourage it; even the most difficult geniuses feel that no one has ever understood their work so well. If you're not creative yourself, you can serve as a vital catalyst for the work of others.

Empty Divinity

A complex and shadowy but unforgettable ecto endo figure was Marilyn Monroe. In her ambiguity, her ability to suggest two contradictory things at once, her lack of definition,

Monroe communicated with her audience at a very deep level. She had the greatest capacity for merging with the fantasies of her fans of almost any movie star who ever lived. Narrow as her acting range was—and it could hardly have been narrower; even at the furthest reach of her ambition she could convincingly play only dizzy blondes—within that range she somehow became whatever her audiences wanted to see in her.

Monroe was not subtle, but she was elusive; there was something secretive about her, something out of reach; you could never get hold of all of her at once. She had the ecto endo's skill at simultaneously expressing opposites: at once frightened and bold, shrewd and helpless, wanton and withdrawn. Monroe's image could be used for one of those projective psychological tests; what you read into her was some aspect of yourself.

Women tended to see her as a guileless child who needed looking after: To actress Hildegarde Neff she was a scared little girl "with short legs and a fat bottom," got up in one of her mother's old evening gowns; to the poet Edith Sitwell she was "a little spring ghost, an innocent fertility daemon." But to Mike Todd she was "the greatest con artist of them all," and to Norman Mailer she was a "general of sex."

She seems to have followed the lethal ecto endo pattern of first burdening others with too much power over her, then turning against them in the suspicion that they were exploiting her. Probably she broke with one Svengali and moved on to the next just at the point where the preceding partnership might have started to pay off. Such vulnerability can be as destructive of others as of itself, and it goes some way toward explaining the ambivalent memories she's left behind, still cutting-sharp after twenty years. An associate producer on several of her films: "Next to her, Lucrezia Borgia was a pussycat." But Natalie Wood: "You don't want anything bad to happen to her. You really care that she should be all right . . . happy."

Well-being for Ecto Endos

The Source of Your Own Supply

You don't trust yourself; it's as though you feel you can't rely on your own inner strength as sufficient to sustain you—a common predicament of low-meso people. You're also the prey of subversive, often self-destructive impulses from within. At its most extreme, this can take the form of a dependence on a combination of alcohol and drugs to wake you up, put you to sleep, and keep you going. But these substances—plus the people you lean on—are less than no help at all in the long run; they leave you as self-mistrustful as ever, and even more desperately reaching for support from without in the next crisis.

The truth is, though, that far more than any inherent weakness, what defeats you is your habit of evasion and procrastination. It's the most insidious enemy of success, but in you it's become such a habitual response to any demand, you're scarcely conscious of it. You manage to get by (just) on a system of always doing something but never what you're supposed to be doing, so that you're late with everything. What it expresses is your resistance to any demands made upon you—even the legitimate demands of your job—and resentment of those who make them, and this in turn masks your dread of not being able to meet those demands.

The ordinary challenges of life will seem overwhelming as long as you remain passive in your dealings with the world. But it's astonishing how even the smallest step toward reversing this tendency—confronting rather than avoiding, taking hold rather than letting slide, moving toward rather than fleeing from—infuses energy and hope, strengthens you for further self-affirming action. The desolate downward spiral can turn into an exhilarating self-confidence if you begin with small acts of courage and self-discipline.

• First, become aware of how often you evade confrontation, consequences, and judgment, and that what you're really doing is judging yourself—as a failure who has to keep dodging and hiding in order to prevent others from recognizing you as such. But this is your own self-appraisal—and incidentally, it's what lurks behind your contempt for the mundane necessary details; you're afraid of completing anything and having it judged less than perfect. This is a dangerous trap for ecto endos: The fantasy is always perfect, the actual result a (relative) failure. But are you content with a life of phantom success?

• You tend to go floating off into daydreams of triumph and applause before you've taken even the first concrete step toward fulfilling your ambitions. The vision of the finished whole inhibits you from making a beginning. Start small; attack each aspect of each problem very specifically. Break the project down into a step-by-step plan, with a timetable. Many a business, even when run by the hardest-headed, has foundered because everybody wanted to concentrate on the big picture and no one was paying attention to the details. Every achievement, every dream realized, can be analyzed into a sequence of small actions. *Analyze* is the key word for you: the cool, detached, impersonal thinking-out of the details of a process. It's a wonderful corrective to dreaming your life away.

• Learn to think quantitatively, to figure costs, plan budgets, allocate your resources—including time. You resist numbers, seeing them as cruel limitations that pin your wings to the ground. But refusing to think in terms of hours and dollars will keep you grounded for sure.

• Bring every task to completion. Don't litter your office with half-completed projects whose idea inspired you for a time but whose execution failed to engage you. Confront your tendency to evade the nitty-gritty; finish what you start. Not being able to rely on yourself to carry anything through is one of your deepest sources of anxiety.

• And curb that impulse to bring your need for love into the workplace. Many of your troubles arise from your demands for and expressions of affection in situations where they don't belong. They're not only inappropriate, they tempt you back into the very passivity you're fighting to free yourself from. The workplace is an arena for action, not for "stroking."

• In your working life, you need to come to terms with a central problem: your low stamina. This doesn't mean making no demands on yourself, but simply that your energy cycle follows a different curve from that of more meso people. It's a shorter curve; your energy tends to come in bursts and to fall off rapidly. You need more frequent and longer periods of rest than mesos do, and you also need to be alone for at least some part of every day. But even a short break helps you to recoup remarkably. What you cannot manage is many consecutive hours at a constant pace. You will not benefit from the advice "Just keep going. You'll soon get your second wind." If you try to do that, you're likely to exhaust yourself, with the recovery taking far longer than the rest break you should have had earlier.

Rest is essential, but change can be almost as effective; you're often more efficient working on two projects at once, switching to the other when you've tired of the first. You also tend to feel livelier as the day wears on, with your spirits peaking in the evening. But what's most important is recognizing that you can recover more rapidly from fatigue and accomplish more if you take frequent short breaks.

Food: Slender Stratagems

Your light-boned body will not accumulate a great weight, but your margin of tolerable excess is small; only a few pounds too many will make the difference between slender curves and pudginess. And carrying those extra pounds around can deplete your slender reserves of energy too.

• Follow the diet tips on pages 51–52. In addition:

• Always start your day with a good breakfast; include both protein and fiber (milk, fruit, cereal). It gives you the energy you need for the day ahead, and the calories you consume in the morning burn off more efficiently than those taken in later in the day.

• Follow breakfast with smaller meals spread throughout your day—midmorning snack, lunch, midafternoon snack, dinner, bedtime—but reduce the amount you eat at each meal. You'll be less hungry than if you concentrate your calories in one or two big meals a day.

• Be sure to include plenty of fluids: soups, juices, tea, coffee. A steady flow of low-calorie liquids can help break a habit of toxic ingestion of alcohol or drugs, and relieve that "empty" feeling—which studies have now shown frequently comes not from hunger but from thirst.

• Few adult Americans, especially women, are getting enough calcium in their diet, but you small-boned ecto endos are particularly vulnerable to the health hazards of a diet that's too low in calcium. And you tend to avoid calcium-rich foods such as milk and cheese because they're also rich in calories. Drink a glass or two of skim milk a day—preferably at night, before going to bed; the calcium is absorbed better when you're lying down. Calcium supplements can help too. And some antacid tablets contain as much as 500 milligrams of calcium per tablet, over half the recommended amount for premenopausal women. Take one or two of these at night too. (But avoid antacids that contain aluminum.)

Exercise: A Body You Can Trust

Central to developing a fitness program for ecto endos is realizing that your feeling of powerlessness arises in large part from a sense of bodily weakness. Self-confidence and optimism can be consciously cultivated, and the most direct approach is to build strength and stamina through structured physical activity. Give yourself a body you can count on, by making a fitness plan and sticking to it. You'll be surprised at how quickly you'll see results if you stay with it—and at how much more confidently you deal with the world when you can trust your own body.

- Your basic regimen should center around swimming, if possible; your natural buoyancy (thanks to your high proportion of fat to muscle) and your small, flexible joints make this the ideal exercise for you. It's your best all-around conditioner and endurance builder, for the water supports you while you develop the muscular strength you need. It's particularly beneficial if you're overweight, because your small skeleton is already overburdened from the excess pounds, and needs the relief from stress to its joints that it gets in the water. Any stroke is fine except for the breast stroke, which puts too much strain on ecto endo backs (but see exercises for weak backs further on).

- Avoid running or jogging; your joints can't take the pounding, even on a resilient running surface. Instead, swim and walk for half an hour on alternate days—or better yet, walk to work and back every day; go swimming two or three times a week.

- The rhythmic togetherness of an aerobics dance class is a perfect workout for you, provided you can find the right one. Stay away from teachers who demand West Point discipline from the outset. Look for one who encourages you to go at your own pace. If at first you can't keep up, just keep moving to the music until you get strong enough to do the routines. It's continuous movement that counts, not precision. So what if you don't reach your target heart rate (see page 107) for a few weeks? If you're out of shape, you've got some catching up to do. Take it easy at first (not *too* easy), and commit yourself to the class three times a week for half an hour. You'll soon see improvement, and it can be a lot of fun.

- Your abdominals and lower back muscles tend to be weak. Calisthenics that pay special attention to these areas will develop strength, prevent injury. For abdominals, try bent-knee curl-ups, and this exercise:

Sit on the floor, knees bent, holding a light weight (one to three pounds) in each hand. Hold the weights just above your stomach and lean back so that your torso is at about a 45-degree angle from the floor. Now pulse up and down there, raising and lowering your torso within about a six-inch range, at the point of maximum contraction of the abdominals. Start with five to ten pulses, increase eventually to a hundred.

• For the back:
   Lie on back, knees bent, feet flat on floor, arms at sides (starting position). Clasp hands around right knee, pull it to chest, hold for a count of five. Repeat five times. Repeat with left leg, then with both together.
   Then, with right hand holding right knee, left hand holding left knee, rock to one side until elbow touches floor, then back to center, then to the other side, lengthening your back a little more each time you rock past the center. Rocking should feel relaxed and easy, a pleasant stretch of the lower back.
   Return to starting position. Keeping lower spine flat against the floor, tighten buttocks. Hold; count to five. Relax. Repeat five times.

• Belly dancing provides a pelvic workout that concentrates on just those areas you need to strengthen: the abdominals and lower back.

• Whichever exercise plan you choose—and it's a good idea to vary your activities, to prevent both boredom and injuries— do not begin with an activity that demands a sustained high output of energy. The point is to build stamina—which with you happens slowly and only with gentle but regular conditioning workouts. Even after you're in condition, however, you'll make better progress if you take frequent short rest breaks. Alternate heavier and lighter workout days, too, and give yourself at least two days a week off (not consecutive ones).

• Do not let yourself be bullied by athletic mesos who assume everyone has as much endurance as they do. Pace yourself according to what your own—not somebody else's—body tells you. If you find that one session of exercise tires you out for the next two days, it's only common sense to cut down to a more comfortable level. Too often you assume that an initial low stamina means one more "failure," decide that physical activity is just another of the multitude of things you're no good at. *Persist.* If you can't swim one lap of the pool, swim across it. If you can't walk a mile, walk a block. Find the level you can maintain three to five times a week without excessive fatigue; then *slowly* increase the duration and intensity of the workout. "No pain, no gain" is another meso myth. If you don't demand immediate dramatic results, but patiently keep at it, you'll be rewarded within a few weeks with a firmer, stronger, slimmer body and a greatly enhanced endurance, self-esteem, and self-confidence.

II.
MESOS:
The People of Will

Mesos are strong, muscular,
assertive, energetic, and ambitious.
Mesos come in three varieties:
balanced mesos, endo mesos, and ecto mesos.

4. BALANCED MESOS:
Rugged and Powerful

Who You Are

Effortless energy and drive characterize you, in whom meso is dominant, with ecto and endo balanced at equal strength below.

Meso means aggressive action. You have massive muscles anchored to heavy bones; your body is sturdy and strong, built for power, endurance, and speed. Your temperament too is geared toward action, especially the kind that pits your strength against an external object or opponent. You were made for hunting and fighting, and even in today's physically softer world you still tend to look upon everything you do as either battle or pursuit. The enemy may be invisible—poverty or ignorance or a cancer cell—but you think instinctively in the language of combat. Both the men and women among you like to move against an objective; you're less interested in cooperation or understanding than in conquering. Most of

91

your metaphors are aggressive: "victory over arthritis"; "task forces in the war against drug abuse"; "headhunting in the corporate jungle."

To meso artists, even creation is a form of warfare; for Picasso, for instance, painting was less a revelation than a rivalry with nature. "A picture used to be the sum of additions," he said. "In my case a picture is a sum of destructions." An endo contemporary of his, Henri Matisse, said, "What I dream of is an art of balance, of purity and serenity . . . an art which might be . . . like a good arm-chair in which to rest from mental fatigue." But to Picasso: "Paintings are not made to decorate apartments; painting is an instrument of war. . . . A good painting—any painting—ought to bristle with razor blades."

The meso body is an efficient instrument for action, with squared shoulders, expanded chest, flat belly, a very straight back, the head held high and assertive, and the face tense—not from apprehension, but set, as in "ready, set, go!" You mesos move with determined vigor and forcefulness. Your center of gravity is high, in the chest, and movements of your shoulders and arms are especially energetic.

You're not necessarily athletic—although you usually do engage, at least while young, in some form of strenuous sport—but you're always highly energized as you go about your daily life, whether from behind a desk or out on a football field. You move fast and decisively, hitting the ground hard when you walk, and your gestures are vigorous and emphatic.

Commanding the Heights

You're comfortable and well oriented in space, and seem almost to find a kind of security in spatial recklessness. You love risks of all kinds, but particularly the continuous spatial risks of mountain climbing, skiing, flying, sky diving. You get a special thrill from climbing to a dizzy peak and perching there, as though ordering your body to balance at such a height gives you mastery over the distances stretching away down below.

You like panoramic perspectives; if possible you'll build

your house on a hill, with spacious rooms not overly furnished and a commanding view. You tend to be somewhat claustrophobic, and you want to be able to see as far off into the distance as possible. The main feature of your house is the view it overlooks, rather than anything in it.

In your surroundings you seek neither comfort nor beauty. Your house is a statement about your status and achievements, not a retreat or an expression of taste. In most ways you live not to express but to impress yourself on the world. You're not interested in objects or possessions except as symbols of wealth or power. You feel suffocated—and will not hesitate to say so—in endo rooms, chock-full of mementos, every surface soft and yielding, perfumed, warm, and close.

You're virtually tireless; five or six hours of sleep a night is usually plenty to ensure a nonstop outpouring of energy during the day. This energy is apparent very young, even before birth. Your mother remembers you as the child who made its presence felt the soonest; you started to move and kick much earlier, more forcibly, and more often.

You develop a strong grip much sooner, too, than other children; you go clambering about with astonishing speed and agility, hanging like a monkey from heights even before you can walk. The motor drive in meso children is imperious; seeing them in action, one usually overestimates their actual age by many months. Typically, you walk long before you can talk; you're exceptionally early walkers, rather late talkers.

You mature early in every way. All your life you look older than your years. Even as a toddler you had a firm set to your face, a steady purposefulness, in striking contrast to the unformed soft blandness of the faces of endo children or the peaked, tentative look, like a just-hatched chick, of small ectos.

This firmness reflects the physical thickness and toughness of your skin and connective tissue, but it also signals a precocious self-sufficiency and sense of direction. Almost from childhood you seem to be fixed, pointed the way you intend to go like a gun emplacement, and you rarely change course. For better or worse, you know who you are and where you're heading before you've left school. During your twenties and thirties you're the ones who set the pace for everyone else, eating up the mileage in the fast lane.

You want three things: action; the feeling of mastery over the external world through acting upon it; and status, the tangible reward for having achieved this mastery. You may not always get what you want, but you're never unsure about your ambitions. Your goals are clear and you advance toward them unhesitatingly:

"I want to go to Harvard, then Harvard Law, and seven years after that I want to be a partner in Sullivan and Cromwell."

"I want to win the Grand Slam in tennis."

"I want to be the youngest senator ever from Connecticut."

"I want to discover the source of the Amazon."

"I want to owe the bank a million dollars before I'm twenty-five."

Woman on the Fast Track

Julie's goals were forced upon her; she had to create herself, and the purposefulness went along with it. She's come a long way from the dusty little Nebraska town where she was born; at thirty-one she heads the legal department in a big Hollywood studio.

Her mother died when she was thirteen, and her father, who didn't believe women should be educated, thought that from then on—or at least until he found himself another wife—Julie ought to stay home and take care of him, the house, and her three brothers. He wouldn't even help her finish high school.

So Julie worked—fought—her way alone, through not only high school but college and then law school, earning every penny, waitressing, typing, working in a cannery, even mowing lawns. It was a lonely struggle that aroused in her a tremendous combative energy, and loaded her with anger and resentment. Julie has always had more drive than anyone else in her family—far more than her brothers, who ironically are the ones who have stayed home: One of them sells used cars, another is the manager of a five-and-dime, and the third is still in junior college. And her long fight to give herself a start in life has confirmed her in an aggressiveness that can be both alarming and magnetic.

When Julie enters a room, it's an event; she radiates vitality, pulls energy toward herself too. Wherever you see a gesticulating, noisy cluster of people at a party, you can be sure that Julie's at the center of it, holding forth outrageously. She's feisty and contentious, but always with warmth and humor, loves nothing more than a good argument; it's a kind of athletic workout. There was never any doubt in her mind that she would become a lawyer, and she was especially looking forward to litigation. What deflected her to corporate practice was the higher status and income.

Julie's sturdy, muscular body bears many superficial scars; it looks battered and hard-used, as it has been. All her life she's been a scrapper; just recently she fought off a mugger at her front door with her briefcase and fists. Like all mesos, she needs the excitement of physical risk to feel fully alive, and the first thing she bought herself when she began making money was a motorcycle, which she races on weekends.

Any number of men who have crossed the path of her brilliant trajectory would have been delighted to act as mentors; one was a celebrated civil-rights lawyer who fell deeply in love with her. But Julie would have none of him, or any of them. She rejects any appeal to the softer emotions that threatens to tie her down. Her great dread is of dependence; since her mother died Julie has never handed any of the responsibility for her future to anyone else—she's pretty sure that their plans for her wouldn't be as big as her own—nor will she surrender any of her momentum. Certainly not to any man. The only thing that can check her stride is to feel powerless, which to her means whatever happens to her not depending solely upon her own decisions and actions.

The Big Sweep

You balanced mesos have a great and well-justified confidence in your ability to manipulate the world of objects in space. Like meso endos, you're consumers of sensation, but you consume it less in the form of sensuous pleasure than as a panoramic registering of all the phenomena of the senses. Your eyes and ears can sweep effortlessly over a vast range of the physical world, taking in every objective detail at once and with equal thoroughness. You make superb scanners, moving rapidly and coolly across a wide sensory field, sharply alert to everything in it that's relevant to your purpose, missing nothing and processing it all with maximum efficiency.

You're a natural at any activity that involves absorbing and classifying large quantities of information for immediate use: piloting a plane, performing complicated surgery, planning military strategy, organizing any sort of industry, devising a new plan for economic distribution. You're in your element when you have to make rapid decisions in which many different factors have to be taken into account. You're most at ease in the world of facts, always eager to go on new fact-finding junkets, to receive fresh briefings and updatings. You're systematic and thorough, excellent at rote learning and memorizing.

You're not easily distracted, either by other people's view-points or by any inner ambivalence. As long as possible, you suppress any consciousness of your inner self that might interfere with the goal-directedness of your energy. Some-times this objectivity gets carried to the point where you experience even your own body as merely another fact out there in the world. One sees this sometimes in athletes, for instance, who in the early stages of illness may notice only that "my batting average kept dropping," or "I couldn't sink those putts the way I used to." Later on they'll say, with equal detachment, "I began to have pounding headaches"—the headaches being merely one more phenomenon of the object world.

When you're this cut off from internal awareness, you can become seriously ill before you have any sense that anything is wrong, because your early warning systems don't get through to headquarters as quickly as they should. This obliviousness, which is an aspect of your insensitivity to pain, explains why mesos so often die suddenly, "without warn-ing." The warnings were there, but they weren't heeded.

You always need to feel that you're in control, and in charge; as subordinates you're uneasy, openly and impatiently waiting for your chance to move into the top spot. You pity the enterprise that doesn't have you as its leader. And it's only those aspects of the world you *can* control that interest you. But some of the most glittering prizes elude capture by force.

Corporate Terrorist

Chuck runs a highly successful business that has become notorious for its rapid turnover in executive staff, although he pays the highest salaries in the industry. Of all his managerial talents, he takes the greatest pride in his skill at spotting creative people and luring them—with sweet talk, golden promises, and extravagant fringe benefits—away from the jobs where they made their reputations. Not, as one might guess, a skill that requires prophetic powers; Chuck raids only strong going concerns for their most productive moneymakers.

His archrival Lionel, a much smaller-scale entrepreneur, has learned to expect an annual descent upon his flock from pirate Chuck. Lionel can't begin to compete with Chuck's glamour and buying power. All he can do, after surveying the wreckage, is sigh and go out scouting once again for the promising but unproven beginners he's so good at discovering and assembling into a productive team. "Sometimes I think my real business is running a nursery for Chuck."

Chuck is fond of expounding his formula for success: "You bring the top talent together, and then you crack the whip to get it outa them." The trouble is, not enough of these prodigies have paid off. When they start working for Chuck, something is lost; they don't come anywhere near producing for him the way they did for Lionel, nor justifying the huge salaries he's paying them. Each successive wonderchild disappoints—fizzles or departs. Chuck can't fathom it. Maybe he's buying merchandise that's a little past its prime? Is sly Lionel slipping him human goods that are on the verge of turning brown around the edges?

Peter, who first blossomed in Lionel's greenhouse, quickly became a spectacular success. For over a year he managed to resist Chuck's blandishments, but finally surrendered. He barely survived what he calls Chuck's "giant threshing machine," and now, three years later, spewed forth gasping for life after Chuck bought out his contract, is disillusioned but wiser:

"Chuck is the kind of guy who sees an orchid growing in the jungle in Brazil, uproots it, and expects it to bloom for him in the Canadian Rockies. Chuck doesn't have a clue that the kind of work people produce for Lionel comes out of a whole environment he creates that encourages the best in you. Chuck thinks he can beat it out of people; he demands originality, but tries to get it by bullying. Then he's surprised when it comes out timid, mechanical, and dead."

Chuck is not sadistic, and he's as dismayed as anyone at his dizzy turnover. But he genuinely believes that people need to be continuously challenged, threatened, pushed and driven and harried—because he himself responds well to such tactics; thick-skinned, he needs a strong exciting impulse. What Chuck is temperamentally incapable of perceiving is that some of the most creative people, whose talents he so heavily depends upon, will only bruise, wilt, or crack under such treatment—and fester with hate.

Of course there's another side: At any aspect of the business in which drive and persistence are the essence, Chuck is superb. It was Chuck who went out with his salesmen and visited in person each and every distributor, showing them exactly how to push a problematical product. He even went to the retail outlets, the drugstores and supermarkets, to check up on sales at the point of purchase. Shoppers became familiar with the sight of Chuck in his big camel's-hair overcoat tugging at a display rack to move it into a more advantageous spot, or down on all fours checking on storage space. Chuck has no idea how to nurture creativity; he knows nothing about the seasons and rhythms of growth. But he's unbeatable at anything requiring only the tireless application of energy and willpower.

Rear-guard Impresarios

As a balanced meso, you need a continual testing of your mettle. Your aspirations are large and never stop expanding; ambition rises along with the rising level of achievement. But you're conventional in the kind of reward you expect; not for you the discriminating appreciation of an elite or the respect of future generations. You want the applause and the prizes *now*. And you want them in the form of certified emblems of status: big money, big cars, ostentatious houses, Learjets, Cartier, Gucci, Jacuzzi—whatever is in fashion (or just a little past the fashion) at the moment.

You'll say, and believe while you're saying it, that what propels you is the desire to make money, give your kids the best of everything, build security for the future. But when you've got it all at last, you're likely to skid into a sudden deep depression. You've discovered that the promise of gold had to be there to give meaning to the contest, but that all the joy was in the contending.

You're often accused of being ruthless materialists, caring only about power and position, and you do go after these things with a single-mindedness that certainly looks like an overwhelming desire to have them. But what you really love is the striving. There's an austerity, an almost heroic purity in you that wants you to be wholly consumed in the act.

The moments others recall with horror are your most treasured memories. Looking back on a life crammed with triumph and riches, you'll recall that you felt most alive "the night I spent with three other guys—all that was left of our patrol—in the cellar of a bombed-out house in the Ardennes. The Krauts had us completely surrounded, and we knew that at dawn they would attack. I was nineteen years old; I had a quart of cognac I'd liberated from the dining room upstairs, and I was sure it was the last night of my life."

Or "the time I was swimming a mile and a half off the Great Barrier Reef, and I saw moving toward me a school of great white sharks."

Or "the night I spent on a ledge twelve thousand feet up a

rock face in Chamonix, in the middle of a blizzard. It was twenty below zero, and my rope had blown away."

Or "the time I flipped my Ferrari completely over not once but twice during a Formula One Grand Prix race."

Some of the most striking features of your temperament are strangely paradoxical. For instance, although you're the most aggressively competitive of any somatotype group, it is not you who determine value. You tend not to set the goals; you're not the people who decide what the name of the game is and how to know if you've won it. All of your energy goes into winning; you can't be expected to lay out the course as well, and fix the direction.

Because of your confidence in manipulating the physical world, you're often thought of as boldly innovative as well, but it's not so. On the contrary, you're usually among the *last* to follow a fashion; it has to have been not only invented but price-tagged before you'll take it up. Innovative people are in closer touch with their inner world of feelings and hunches, of dreams and fantasies. They seem to be responding to the current not of what is, but of what's about to be. They sense and seize upon what has not yet materialized, is still subterraneanly preparing itself. Your meso objectivity, by concentrating exclusively upon what is obvious to common sense and has already been validated by others, blocks your awareness of latent potential.

It's the other side of your mastery of the exterior; because your focus is so relentlessly outer-directed, you're blind, relatively, to what is within, or not yet. Two questions you never ask: "How do I feel about it?" and "What does it mean?" Ignoring them gives you great power over the immediate and tangible, but it also means that you tend to lack originality. The people who "make it new" are those who are dissatisfied with the status quo. Just because you can deal with reality so successfully, your imagination is often underdeveloped. You don't need to construct alternative possibilities, fantasy worlds of desire fulfilled; you can be master in this world.

You're among the least hedonistic people, the least sensual; you rarely do anything just because it feels good. When

Stravinsky was asked by an interviewer how he could tell when he was on the right track with a composition, he replied, "I know when it's good by the pleasure I feel." You'd be scandalized at the notion of letting desire be your guide.

Humility and Hierarchy

Another paradox: While you're the great adventurers of the physical world, you shy away from journeys within, psychological risk-taking. You will happily invite death by freezing at the North Pole, suffocating on the moon, or boiling in a cannibal stew, but you'll seldom say yes to an invitation to a voyage into your own interior; the prospect of diving into the uncharted territory of your own mind is dismaying. A meso who has circumnavigated the earth alone in an open boat will say in awe to a writer, "How can you face that blank sheet of paper?" You dislike wandering or wondering goallessly; it's hard for you to empty yourself of ego or of will, nor can you imagine wanting to do so.

Or indulging in the free play of curiosity, just "fooling around." That means no direction, activity with no specific purpose—and therefore no clear-cut winners and losers. You probably can't even take a walk without wanting to lop five minutes off the house record for a hike to the next cow pasture and back. Aimless free play threatens you on many levels. In free play there is no leader, and also no telling where a new idea will come from. It could come from the janitor, or a four-year-old child, or a joke, or even from one's wife. Free play is fundamentally subversive, a menace to hierarchy—which to you is the basis of all social order.

In meso institutions—the paradigm being the army, and including corporate structures in business and industry, chains of command in hospitals and political parties, the police, the church, the Mafia—power moves from the top down through fixed ranks of decreasing authority. Empires are meso structures; loose federations of equals are not, nor is any form of democracy.

Which results in a third paradox: You mesos, the living principle of aggressiveness, are at the same time of all people the most submissive and humble—to those more powerful.

Power being your sole determinant of value, it defines and limits all relationships. A meso will genuflect to a power superior to his own with a deference that is close to fatalistic. You all want to be Number One, but if that's impossible, then you need to know that you're Number Thirty-two. Your sense of hierarchy commands your strongest allegiance; the structure is almost more important than your own place in it. You can stand not winning; what you cannot bear is that the race itself be questioned. And if the race is not always to the swift, what's the point of having a race at all?

Some kinds of questions are intolerable to you: those to which there is no immediate right answer. "What's it all about?" "Is it worth it?" "Is this the way I want to spend the rest of my life?" The answers to such questions must come from a small voice within, and you tend to be deaf to messages from your interior; in fact, you resist acknowledging that the subjective realm even exists. But it isn't so much that the inner world of feeling, intuition, and imagination isn't real to you as that, in the competition for your attention, the outer world of facts and things always wins. Whatever your own inner voice may be saying is never more than half-consciously attended to, so impatient are you to escape from that shadowy and suspect region into the bright light of "reality."

But you're dependent upon that reality remaining predictable and steady. In periods of transition in your own life, or of upheaval in the world around you—when reality is no longer fixed but subject to sudden shocks and reversals, and survival requires a feel for the unpredictable—you're likely to be as confused and lost as you were confident and bold in more stable times. A meso mogul faced with compulsory retirement at an age when he's just beginning to realize his possibilities will feel as helpless as a child.

When Lee Iacocca was forced out as president of Ford at fifty-five, Gail Sheehy reported, "Having lived by the sword, it would be one thing if he could die by it in the marketplace at the peak of his power. But what it looked like was that he would have to bow out into nothingness."

What troubled Iacocca most was a feeling of dislocation. He told Sheehy: "My whole life has been: here are the problems, put 'em on a piece of paper, set a timetable, and then go to 'em! But you go to something like this— . . . So what *do* you wanna do? . . . If I have a fear, it's what do you do when you've been embroiled in an activity like this, and it suddenly stops?"

Well-Being for Balanced Mesos

Power from Dreams

A satisfactory answer to a question like Iacocca's can come only from a collaboration between the conscious and the unconscious minds, but mesos are wary of anything not wholly subject to conscious control. You're interested only in what the surface of your mind tells you; the buried half had best stay buried. But you cut yourself off from it at your peril. The claims of the subjective world are real and equally imperious; ignoring them can mean not only spiritual death, but failure even in the world you want to rule.

It's that subjective realm that confers value, tells you what's *worth* fighting for. If you're deaf to its voice, you're only a machine—a formidable one, no doubt, but all too easily made the unthinking tool of someone with a stronger inner purpose. Such, for instance, was the fate of the German generals under Hitler. Their command of objective reality was total; then they were confronted by this fanatic who was able to communicate directly with the dark fantasies of the German people. As Albert Speer, architect to the Third Reich, remarked, "The military men had all learned to deal with a wide variety of unusual situations. But they were totally unprepared to deal with this visionary." Against that kind of power they were helpless.

One way of opening a channel to that other realm is through the act of contemplation. This is very difficult for you, because it means receiving something mentally without judging it or acting upon it. To look at a painting, to listen to music in a state of passive expectancy, of alert receptiveness, without doing anything about it, merely experiencing it—this is an ability you've very likely never developed. And not because you "haven't time" for anything that isn't going to advance your career or make money for you, but because in fact you're actually afraid of opening yourself up, of making yourself available to an experience that might change *you*. You're so used to doing things to the world, acting upon or against it, that reversing the direction of your energy feels like an assault upon all your habits. And the state of suspended judgment, of uncertainty, the mind open to letting something new happen to it, can be disconcerting, even frightening. But it's a state of being that, just *because* you resist it, you need to learn how to enter.

- Listen for ten minutes to a piece of serious music; stand for five silent minutes before a picture; read a chapter in a serious novel without dismissing anything you find there. If it seems boring, then make a case for it: What is the writer (composer, painter) trying to do? Why did he choose to do it this way? If you don't understand it or think it's dopy, assume that the deficiency is in you. If it's a classic, why has it lasted?

Being able to enter a contemplative state confers the gift of "negative capability," which the poet Keats thought the essential trait of "a man of achievement": being able to live "in uncertainty, mysteries, doubts, without any irritable reaching after fact and reason." The advantage of being able to live with doubt and uncertainty, of not having to rush to a decision as soon as conflicting claims present themselves, is that the resolution, when it does come, is arrived at with the help of the unconscious mind, which in its way sees more and sees deeper into any situation.

Of course, most of your daily life does require only the immediate solutions provided by conscious reasoning; the point is that these deeper levels ought to be accessible to you, not sealed off, where they become a source of fear and danger. Often it's our dreams that tell us what it is we're ignoring, to our loss.

• Keep a large blank book by your bedside, and as soon as you wake up, write down your dreams, whatever you can remember of them. What's likely to happen is that, as though encouraged by this chance to be heard, your unconscious will start pouring out dreams, and your dream life will immediately become much more richly detailed than it has ever been, more colorful and eventful, and writing the dreams down will be not a chore but a pleasure—at times very exciting.

Don't try to interpret or understand the dreams; just register them, become an audience for this other self, and see where it wants to take you. If any associations with your waking life occur to you, write those down, too, but don't decide too quickly that a dream is, for instance, "about" that argument with your brother the night before, and nothing more. Some such event may have triggered the dream, but it has its own life too; the point of this exercise is not to dismiss that independent life. Understanding will come naturally, in its own time, as your two selves become more integrated. The benefits are unpredictable, but will certainly be profound. You'll find that not only your dreams but your waking experience, too, becomes more vivid, more intensely lived, in quite unexpected ways, and that your whole life becomes enriched and deepened.

It takes an unusual courage for mesos deliberately to elicit the unknown and therefore potentially unmanageable in themselves, but by cutting yourself off from it you risk becoming shrunken and stiff and narrow, way before your time. You need to expand your concept of enjoyable risk to include the deeper levels of your own mind. Can you accept the challenge?

Food: Open Channels

The most serious health hazard threatening you as a group is cardiovascular disease, still the number one killer. The meso body build is in itself a significant risk factor in fatal heart attacks among young and middle-aged men and women.

Both diet and exercise play an important, perhaps decisive,

role in the prevention of heart disease. The American diet is one of the highest in the world in fat, especially animal fat, found in such foods as milk, eggs, cheese, butter, and meat. A cherished meso conviction is that red meat builds heroes. This delusion originates in a bit of magical thinking: To acquire the power you desire (and fear), kill and eat the flesh of the animal who possesses it. But those animals will get you in the end. Steak, no matter how you slice it, is 50 percent fat. Animal fats raise the level of blood cholesterol, the substance that clogs the arteries of heart attack victims, and a number of long-term studies point to our fat-soaked diet as one of the culprits. Why mesos are especially at risk is not yet fully understood, but since in mesos the connective tissue, which includes blood vessels, is heavier than in ectos and endos, it may be that meso arteries are thicker-walled to begin with, with a narrower channel for the blood, and that therefore a life-threatening constriction occurs sooner from cholesterol buildup along those walls.

• Get most of your protein from vegetable sources, such as whole grains and nuts (see the chart on page 70 for fat-free vegetable-protein combinations).

• Eating fish, especially fatty saltwater fish, can cut the risk of heart attack in half, thanks to their high level of fatty acids that reduce blood cholesterol. The varieties that protect include Atlantic mackerel, sardines, herring, bluefish, rainbow trout, lake whitefish, sablefish, squid, bluefin tuna, and pink, chinook, red, and coho salmon. So make fish your main source of animal protein; have it at least twice a week.

• Olive oil also protects by lowering blood cholesterol. Nor does it carry other risks, as polyunsaturated vegetable oils do. Heart disease is rare among people whose dietary fat is primarily olive oil, such as Italians and Greeks. Wherever possible, use olive oil in preference to butter or vegetable oils.

Exercise: Playing for Your Life

Mesos need regular exercise, not only to protect your hearts—evidence is overwhelming that inactivity contributes to heart disease and exercise protects against it—but also because your bodies are built for strenuous physical use and, if they don't get it, deteriorate fast.

Your outer-directedness often leads you to ignore, or never hear, your body's early warning signals of distress. Since an illness may have progressed rather far before you first experience pain or discomfort, it's imperative that you have regular medical checkups. Don't wait until you suspect something is wrong. So if your life has been sedentary for more than a year, be sure to get a medical okay before embarking on any exercise regime.

• You can excel at virtually any sport, but your program should include at least half an hour of aerobic workouts three or four times a week. Aerobics conditions the cardiovascular system, and is therefore the most important part of any meso fitness program. In practice, aerobics means *continuous* movement of the legs; working those big leg muscles is what taxes the heart enough to condition it. Such exercise includes running, jogging, walking, cycling, cross-country skiing, and swimming, but usually not tennis, football, or baseball (too much stopping and starting).

• Choose one of the above, or vary them day by day, but begin with twenty minutes or a half hour three times a week, build up to half an hour to an hour four or five times a week.

• Maintain a heart rate that falls within a target zone, to be computed as follows: Subtract your age from 220. (If you're thirty, that would be 190—your predicted maximum heart rate.) Your target zone would then be the range that falls between 65 percent and 80 percent of that number; in this case, between 124 and 152 beats per minute. Your aim is to reach that zone and stay in it for at least twenty minutes four times a week.

• When you first begin an aerobics program, take your pulse every five or ten minutes to make sure you're staying within that zone. Frequent pulse testing is especially valuable for mesos as feedback training; learning to relate your internal sensations to the objective fact of a pulse rate helps you develop a more sensitive awareness of what your body is telling you. Never exceed a rate at which you can comfortably carry on a conversation (the "talk test").

• Stretches, warmups, and cool-downs are vital. Failure to stretch and warm up can cause injuries, and ignoring the cool-down is even more dangerous: Blood tends to pool in the legs if you stop exercising suddenly, temporarily reducing the blood supply to the heart and brain, which can cause not only dizziness and fainting but, in a susceptible person, even cardiac arrest. When you come to the end of your aerobics workout, don't stop all at once. Keep moving; walk briskly, or if you're swimming, move your arms and legs in the water for at least three minutes.

• Stretches should emphasize the area that will be stressed by your sport: Stretch your hamstrings if you'll be jogging, arms and shoulders for tennis or squash.

• Warmups should consist of jumping jacks, running in place, and a slow round of the activity you're about to engage in. Swim or jog a few easy laps before you go all out. "Warmups" literally raise the temperature of the muscles by increasing their blood supply, preparing them for the demands you're about to make on them.

• Jumping rope provides an excellent fast aerobic workout for busy mesos—you can even do it in a hotel room. But it raises the heart rate very quickly, so start slowly and be sure to monitor your pulse carefully.

• You risk becoming rigid as you get older, feeling comfortable only within an increasingly narrow range of activities and ideas. You need to work at remaining (or becoming) flexible, keeping your range of options as broad as possible, and not letting yourself be imprisoned by a premature stiffening of your mental and physical muscles. You can work on this through your body, by including in your fitness program a strong emphasis on flexibility and body awareness, two areas you're likely to ignore. To you the body is an instrument of aggression; you prefer "killer" contact sports or those that stimulate your combative energy. You'd benefit from training in sports that encourage another attitude toward aggression, developing balance, suppleness, and inner awareness—such as aikido, the Oriental martial art that makes use of flowing movement, precision of timing, and the momentum of the aggressor against himself; trains you to see both yourself and your attacker as parts of a single whole; and has as its aim an ultimate harmonious oneness with nature.

• If you've been out of condition for a while, don't expect your body to perform suddenly at peak level. Don't make abrupt, high surges of demand on it which it is not conditioned to meet. You tend to be impatient with your body—which can be dangerous. Reconditioning must be gradual, and not self-punitive. Learn to play by your body's own rhythms; develop a feeling for its needs and capacities. It's willing and strong and will readily respond, provided you don't try to pummel and pound it into obedience.

5. ENDO MESOS:
Tough and Resilient

Who You Are

An incessant, ebullient vitality characterizes you endo mesos, in whom meso, the extraverted component of energy and action, is dominant; endo, the extraversion of feeling, is the secondary strength; and ecto, which inhibits the expression of both feeling and action, is the weakest of the three. You're the most exuberantly energized of any somatotype group. You're the steamrollers, seemingly made of solid rubber, sturdier and more durable than other people, and the harder you get thrown, the higher you bounce.

You're usually found on the winning side of any enterprise, and the secret of your success is simple: Nothing stops you. Nothing. Once in motion—and you're always in motion—not fear, nor guilt, nor good taste, nor caution, nor fatigue, nor self-doubt, nor virtually any external obstacle can halt or even slow your momentum. You roll along with the force of a juggernaut, and everybody else had better either get out of your way or jump aboard.

"Keep moving" is your rule of life. Better to move in the wrong direction than not at all. Action is life, and life, action; stillness is death. If you just keep going, you'll eventually get *somewhere*. So imperious is this impulse that many of you would rather play in a crooked game, one you know is cruelly rigged against you, than not play at all. Winning matters, of course, but just because you're losing is no reason to pull out; winning is important, but it comes a long, long way behind being part of the action.

Here's a man with a small, struggling business trying to

reason with his endo meso partner after an unbroken series of disasters:

"Four strikeouts is enough for me; I quit."
"Five is when we hit it."
"But we screw up every time. Something new is always going wrong."
"See? We don't make the same mistake twice."
"If we haven't got it by now, we never will."
"We're just getting the hang of it; next time is the payoff."

In all your undertakings, you're powered by an enormous and indestructible optimism. Some people keep moving because they don't know what else to do, or out of fear of collapsing if they stop; others keep busy in order to hold their inner demons at bay. Not you. You're borne along on great waves of gusto, surging ahead in sublime confidence that everything will go your way. Somewhere you know as well as anybody that you won't always win, but you vigorously thrust all such thoughts aside.

Hattie heads one of the mayor's emergency task forces. A big woman who wears big hats ("so you won't notice m' hips"), she was brought in because she listens to no nay-sayers, her bulldozer energy and outlook of total positiveness mowing down any opposition. You can always hear her coming, with her roar of laughter and pounding walk, and her voice that's both a growl and an embrace. She's noisy, insensitive, huge-hearted, and she does what she has to do to get the job done, without regard for anyone's feelings and from the largest of motives. She doesn't see the point of being fearful or small-scale—either do it right (i.e., generously) or don't do it at all.

She regularly works fourteen-hour days, and says the only hard part about her job is that "most people are just looking for an excuse to say no, because then they won't have to get up off their butts. 'That'll never work,' they say. 'Uh-uh, you'll never get anywhere with that one, Hattie. Just file and forget it.' Or else, 'It's a great idea, but it's not for us.' And they're so *delighted* when they can say no. And so relieved! They put all their juice into the no. They're in love with the no! I used to think all you had to do was make people see how important this work was and they'd fall all over themselves trying to help. With ninety percent of them I've learned to count myself lucky if they just don't get in my way."

Compared with Hattie the rest of us live bowed down in a state of chronic mild depression. When her husband and her son were both killed in a terrible accident two years ago, Hattie had to fight hard to keep going—but of course she did. And while she has some "bad days," on the other days she's her old self. It would never be her way to live permanently subdued in a gray haze of grief. Like a balloon, her natural state is up.

"Keep On Rollin'"

You're unsinkable, impervious to blows from fate or foes. The world can sit on you, step on you, stamp on you, but it cannot squash you or keep you down. You have a kind of innate shock absorber that can take any amount of punishment; you always bounce back, cheerful and ready for anything. No disgrace—failure, bankruptcy, prison—leaves any lasting mark; life never seems to wear you down or out. You come bobbing right back up again, tireless, shameless, confident as ever, percolating with a thousand ideas and schemes, nine hundred and ninety-nine of them terrible, and wholly in love with every one.

Most of these schemes consist of new ways of rearranging and exploiting the stuff of the world. You think concretely and quantitatively. Your grasp of the immediate and the tangible is complete, and little else enters your calculations. Psychologically you stay in close touch with your infant self; all your life you care most about the things you can touch, smell, eat, squeeze, pound.

Like all extraverts, you have a strong sense of process, of how to get the job done. If you're an innovator, it's more likely to be in the realm of new methods, new technologies, rather than in deciding what, basically, to do. A surprising number of the men among you are enthusiastic cooks, and you'll analyze the process of preparing a veal scaloppine with the same absorption in the details as you'll discuss new techniques for smelting copper.

You like to keep as many balls spinning in the air as possible. Instinctively you play percentages; "Keep rollin'" is your motto. Quantity always wins out in the end. Try enough things, and a few of them are bound to pay off. Often you'll win big, then lose it all, then win it all back again. Energy is your chief resource; you refuse to quit, and all that activity generates luck.

Your energy and audacity always keep pushing you to take on more and more, never to pare down, cut back; you're naturally expansive rather than contractile. You're the gutsy operators who can assume heavy responsibilities in a dozen different directions at once and never feel any strain; who can withstand, with no threat whatever to your inner security, all the buffetings of fate, the drastic veerings and reversals of fortune that befall those who take big chances. In your structural toughness, which combines strength with heavy insulation, you're built to take risks. You're hard-muscled, rugged-boned, thick-skinned, with a still thicker layer of subsurface fat that cushions you from shocks and abrasions. And since your emotional control center is buried so deep inside, you're virtually nerveless, impervious to surface disturbances of any kind.

This imperturbability is what makes heroes. You drive straight ahead to the point, the job to be done, eyes firmly fixed on the goal. You have the heart that's rock-steady in a crisis, "holding the line," going in without a tremor of hesitation to battle or the rescue. It's you endo mesos who keep returning to the white-hot center of the holocaust in a munitions factory explosion to search for survivors; who descend again and again thousands of feet down a mine shaft in a rickety one-man bucket on a chain, carrying one by one the victims of a cave-in back to the surface in your arms; who tirelessly and without flinching nurse the hopelessly and horribly mutilated.

Risks and Kicks

The other side of endo meso imperviousness is an insensitivity to stimuli that pushes you to seek stronger and stronger sensations. You need a lot of excitement in order to feel fully alive. You're especially invigorated by risk, and are often inveterate gamblers. Not the frenetic, compulsive type of gambler; you have too much control for that, and you don't have the addict's drive toward ruin. You play at the big table and will plunge heavily, but you always know what you're doing. You're mistaken a lot of the time, but you're not possessed by the will to lose, the urge to be abruptly lifted up, then as suddenly flung down; and you have none of the compulsive gambler's essential passivity. You're your own sole agent in everything you do. Nobody coerces you; either your own will is wholly behind it, or you don't do it at all. One never senses the presence in you of any inner drive that's at odds with the conscious will, the ego.

But you do need the fillip, the kick, of a small or large risk that lends color to life. And the easiest way to get this is by gambling, from a little flutter on a hot stock tip or a couple of hundred on the Super Bowl to staking your all on the commodities market. Literally thick-skinned, you need constantly to fend off boredom—the boredom of the consitutionally insensitive, for whom the ordinary stresses of living don't offer enough excitement.

You need strong physical sensations too. You're great consumers of tobacco, especially strong cigars—even the women among you enjoy the sting of cigarillos—and you like sharp, pungent flavors. Your Tex-Mex chili is seven-alarm; at a Chinese or Indian restaurant, you order the pepperiest Szechuan dishes, the most gullet-searing vindaloo curries.

You mature early; most of your attitudes and values are set by adolescence. After that you don't often develop in a new direction, but simply expand in the old ones, doing more and more, on a bigger and bigger scale, of exactly what you've done before. Once in motion, it's almost impossible for you to change course. *Innovation* to you usually means extension and expansion, more of the same, rather than any new departure. An endo meso movie producer about to release his fifth disaster film in a row will brag about his creative boldness if he's used a typhoon this time, or tried out a new leading man; the slightest variation in the formula is pioneering. More often the boldness consists of aggressively seeking new markets, or a modification in the manufacturing process, rather than any new basic idea.

You're both audacious and conservative, fearless adventurers who never cut completely loose from your moorings. At a playground the endo meso child is conspicuous for his physical self-confidence, which by the age of three or four is already fully developed. There he is at the center, wherever the crowd is thickest, running things. He ignores his mother completely for long stretches, never looking in her direction (although no matter how far away she is, he senses instantly if she moves). Then some obscure need to reestablish contact sends him staggering over to the bench where she's sitting, to cling to her leg for a few minutes, maybe even climb into her lap. But he doesn't linger there for long. Suddenly he's off again, digging, building, demolishing, chasing, organizing, bossing, yelling.

"Prudence Is an Ugly Old Maid"

Even the most buccaneering daredevils among you are never loners; in fact, you usually fear and distrust the real eccentrics. You're wary of anyone who has no discernible roots, suspicious of drifters, seekers, questioners. You're agglomerative, faithful to the idea at any rate of the family. You're never political revolutionaries, either; you need a stable social structure in which to operate. If you're discontented, it's not with "the system" per se so much as your own place in it; you don't want a new pie, just a bigger piece of this one. A person should be firmly anchored in the world, you feel, with enough people dependent on him, and enough deals going, to have a stake in the outcome of events.

But although you tend to be politically conservative, you do venture—you're the quintessential entrepreneurs—and you have terrific tenacity, the courage to hang in and keep forging ahead against the odds. You despise caution, restraint, thrift, agreeing with William Blake: "Prudence is an ugly old maid wedded to incapacity." Your instinct is always to do rather than refrain from doing. To "Why?" your reply is "Why not?" Such relentlessly positive thinking gives off an energy that like a magnetic field pulls people and projects toward you.

Those projects are always highly concrete. Mathematicians, physicists, or fantasists, who are bent on proving that the "real" world is an illusion, almost always have a hefty dose of ecto in their makeup; rarely are they dominant mesos or endos. You frequently have a good "head for figures," but you'll use it for constructing things in the world like airplanes or apartment complexes. You're never theoreticians; you're very happy with the world of appearances just the way it looks and feels and tastes and smells, provided you can grab a giant-sized helping of it when it's being parceled out.

You seem born to flourish in boom times only, but when the crash comes, and the crunch, and everybody else is running scared and cutting back, you're the one who sees that if nobody can afford a new car anymore, the thing to get into is the used-car market; that discounted goods sold off pushcarts in the street will attract buyers who can't afford to shop in department stores; that entertainment has to become colorful, escapist, and cheap—and you clean up then too. Somehow you always seem to scramble back up when the wise and sober have gone under.

You have an overmastering urge to feel independent, hating any restriction on your freedom of action. Whether or not you're actually your own boss is less important than the sensation of being free and in charge. Many endo meso men who seem to be trapped in dead-end blue-collar labor actually prefer it. A trucker or a crane operator will tell you, "Man, when I'm rollin' along in the middle of the night, or swingin' high over the town in the cab of that crane, I feel like I'm king of the whole country, far as I can see."

That he's paid an hourly wage and owns nothing matters less than the feeling of autonomy. Most of these men would rather work for a boss who leaves them alone than run their own business, if that means constant headaches with the help or having to cater to stockholders. The knowledge that the business is theirs on paper can't compensate for the feeling of constraint.

Hustling Showman

You're often built on an opulent scale, and those of you who make it big like to set up shop in imperial headquarters, as in the old white-elephant mansion of some bygone tycoon. You go for the imperial style in decor, too, with sunken marble bathtubs that would accommodate a water polo team and drawing rooms the size of ballrooms.

Eddie ("Big Ed") is a promoter with such an office. At the moment, on this spin of fortune's wheel, Eddie is in a turn-of-the-century Italianate town house off Fifth Avenue in New York, reigning in the tapestry-hung *salone*, a field marshal ensconced behind his ornate Renaissance desk. This is his command station; ranged over it are five white telephones that are never idle, whose push buttons he fingers like a keyboard. Eddie is primarily a "packager" of spectacles and sporting events, but he likes to think of himself as a "communicator," and from this action control center he talks to the world. He'd like best to have you there in front of him so he could shake you into submission, but he does just as well vocally, assaulting the telephone lines with a tornado of talk, cajoling, bullying, wheedling, threatening.

Eddie is rough and capable of violence, but he's not cruel. He has a heart; he "takes care" of people. For years he's kept afloat a raft of relatives, hangers-on, freeloaders, and indigent drinking cronies, some of whom are always to be found lounging about the *salone*. Eddie won't foreclose or evict if he can possibly help it. He always gets a percentage, takes a little advantage, but he's not interested in destroying anybody; he commits many kindnesses to keep the game going. In his own life it's caviar one day, franks and beans the next, and as long as either keeps flowing, no one will be turned away from his table. Most of his rescue operations are conducted privately; sensitive in little else, he has a delicate consideration of the pride of others. Otherwise his life is one glaring public display of effrontery and hustle.

How well he knows that appearances matter more than
truth—that they *create* the truth. Without a nickel to his name
he'll rent a limousine to impress a prospective backer, and
return with the capital he needs. He spends many thousands
on his clothes. "Act it, and you'll believe it," he says. "And if
you believe it, *they* will."

"Okay, Eddie, but it's only a show, don't forget that."

"*Only* a show!" he shouts, incredulous. "What the hell does
that mean? The show is the whole ball of wax!"

He has a way of surrounding every situation, taking
command of it from all sides so that whatever the outcome,
it's his personal victory. He loves to put you on the spot with
belligerent quizzes. If you can't answer, he wins, of course,
but if you can, he wins too. He's forever jabbing a finger into
your chest, thrusting his face into yours, and demanding,
"Okay, smartass. Who was the biggest underdog ever to win a
heavyweight title fight?"

"It was Braddock, Eddie, at ten to one against Baer in
'thirty-five."

"That's . . . RIGHT!" he shouts exultantly, beaming, looking around to collect the applause. What great tests he comes
up with, and what brains he's gathered around him! What a
lucky world this is, to have him in it!

Eddie's judgment of people is astute. He can usually spot a
loser, a fake, a cheat, a four-flusher, a ball-buster—any
obviously or subliminally destructive force—within seconds
of meeting him or her. He has no analytic capacities whatever,
but something better: a vast experience. Eddie has rolled with
so many punches, survived so many disasters, lived a life so
crammed with incident that he can recognize the stigmata of
just about every form of human deviance—without for a
moment being able to identify them by name. "Stay away
from that guy—he's a shitload of bad news."

"What makes you say that, Eddie? He's got a great track
record."

"One'll get you five that track record is a phony—I know
that type."

"Which type is that?"

"The type with a great phony track record that'll rip you off
down to your underwear."

The Momentum of Money

You endo mesos are seldom dependent upon or even influenced by your surroundings. You don't look outside yourself for support of any kind; your exuberance is powered from within. And you've probably been this way from birth, or close to it. Your relationship to the past is complex. On the one hand, you're always trying to move away from it, clinging to nothing, especially played-out romances, but anything else as well that has lost its capacity to amuse you. You wear people out fast, especially recent acquaintances. But you're fiercely loyal to old friends and spouses; your divorce rate is low. And you have a strong sense of family. You may stray very far, and the family itself may become widely strewn, but nobody ever falls through the meshes for good.

You like to think money can buy anything. After making a fortune in business, many of you become heads of foundations. And you never can see why the laying out of money—amassing the biggest names in the most lavish physical plant with the most ambitious endowment program—doesn't guarantee a cure for cancer, on a timetable set by you. "If we can put men in space, we can lick the Big C," you assert confidently. You never really grasp the distinction between the refinement of existing technology and a wholly new idea. And in the absence of an animating idea or theory, you tend to bull ahead anyway, and what you end up getting for your money is a colossal architectural pile in which nothing is happening. Which is baffling, because why aren't idea people like ketchup bottles? You ought to be able to extract whatever you need from them if you just shake them hard enough.

It's rarely you who have the ideas. You can market a new invention better than anyone, but the act of creation, that first faltering step in the dark, is usually taken by an ecto. You'd like to think that the best way to generate ideas is to keep jetting talented people from one international conference to another, because all that takes is motion, and you yourselves hate sitting still. Deep down, though, you usually know better. You know that what you've got to hope for is the luck and the savvy to get hooked up with the real thing, unprepossessing as it may appear, and then leave it alone. It's difficult for you to accept this, but some memorable partnerships have been based on just such an uneasy teaming of creativity with executive energy; think, for instance, of General Leslie Groves and Robert Oppenheimer, the endo meso army man and the ecto visionary.

The mysterious, erratic quality of creativity is associated in the minds of endo meso men with the female principle; "real men" aren't geniuses, as a rule. And women, representing generativity, are, like all creative people, unfathomable and tricky, even treacherous, to deal with. They're mettlesome, contrary creatures, guided by wayward and illogical instincts of their own. Handling them requires a special skill, the sort of knack it takes to manage animals. Endo mesos are monogamous in the sense that there's only one wife at home in charge of the household, but they often feel that a man has a right to as many mistresses (or "ladies"—they never use the unisex "lover") as he can "take care of." Nobody tells a guy he can keep only one horse, right? You can own as many horses as you can keep stabled, fed, and exercised. Why shouldn't the same go for women?

The Double-H Team

Some men are attracted to women as Otherness, but women who are themselves endo mesos appeal more strongly to another type of endo meso man, the kind who wants companionship from a woman—not his complement but a female counterpart, a wife who can keep up with him. And the two of them can make a formidable team.

Such is the team of Heinrich (Hank) and Deirdre Hammerschlag, owners of Hammerschlag Construction Company and the Double-H Ranch just outside Phoenix. Twenty-five years ago Deirdre reached the semifinals at Wimbledon, and she still has a bone-crushing handshake. Since then she's taken up golf. A little more buxom today but as powerful as ever, Deirdre is an imposing presence, with eyes as blue and clear and hard as the Arizona sky, strong white teeth, a grin that splits her burnished-mahogany face into deep, leathery crevasses, and a voice of bourbon and barbed wire.

Deirdre has the gift of instinctive command over dogs, horses, children, and men. She's a full partner with Hank in the construction company, which builds shopping centers and retirement homes throughout Arizona and New Mexico. Hank consults closely with her on every aspect of project development, from site appraisal to financing to on-site supervision of the crews. But her special domain is the ranch: thirty thousand head of Hereford, many of whom behave like members of the family. Stick your head out of your bedroom window in the rambling Hammerschlag ranch house, and you're likely to find yourself face to face with a curious steer.

The house is Sunbelt Feudal style, its walls garnished with Deirdre's trophies and studded with the horns of bygone cattle, with ceilings made of old Southern Pacific railroad ties and a dining-room table of polished redwood planks that seats thirty. The rooms are big, to accommodate the Olympian-scale Hammerschlags, who nevertheless are rarely to be found in the same one. They both take up a lot of space and are not particularly strong on togetherness, certainly not during the working day, when Deirdre is usually out with the ranch foreman and Hank is at a construction site. But whenever the two of them are at home at the same time, they're likely to be bellowing companionably back and forth from opposite ends of the house.

Well-being for Endo Mesos

Power Through Repose

What you endo mesos need most is to develop the capacity for stillness, for repose. Where meso endos flood the moment with feeling, you bludgeon it with industrial-strength energy. This is just the ticket when it comes to getting things done. But when the object is encounter, meeting another person in an even exchange or on his or her terms, you tend to steamroll over him, leaving him flattened and you having learned nothing. Learning to receive, to reverse the direction of those waves of radiant energy, to take in, to listen and observe in silence—these are capacities you've probably never valued, perhaps have even despised. But a sensitivity to others, an awareness of what's really going on in them, is a prerequisite for success in any field that involves working with people—which is pretty much all the fields you're likely to be interested in.

You are probably used to being the noisiest, most outgoing person around from as far back as you can remember, have never known what it feels like *not* to be giving out. But when you're incapable of receiving, you've reduced by half your range of possible human response—and the other half becomes increasingly coarsened. If you're always living at a shout, you become psychologically deafened, more and more numbed in your capacity to listen even to your own inner voices, let alone to anyone else, and you have to shout louder and louder just to hear yourself. If you can deliberately cut back on the energy and decibel level of your output, and try going over to the receiving end, you begin to restore some flexibility and vibrancy to your outgoingness, as you realize that you don't have to drown out everybody else to make yourself heard.

Those sensory receivers have probably atrophied from lack of use, always overridden by your transmitter. Try this:

• The next time you enter a room in which there are one or two other people sitting quietly, resist the temptation to disturb the peace, to shake things up. Keep your voice down, *below* theirs; if they're not talking, you remain silent too. Reduce your outgoing energies to a level you will undoubtedly feel is far too subdued, and direct them instead to receiving emanations from the others. You'll be consciously reversing a lifelong tendency to give out, which will not be easy, but try it as an experiment. See how it feels. Pale? Lifeless? Dull? Perhaps that's the way you've been making the others feel—the people you've been outshouting all this time.

• Now try to sense the state of your body. Do you feel that the muscles of your upper torso, shoulders, neck, and face are set, braced to charge forward, to overpower any opposing energy? Can you let go of those muscles little by little, consciously relaxing your face, your neck, dropping your shoulders, breathing not strenuously from your upper chest but loosely, from deep in your belly? Can you let your body be loose, easy, quiet, and receptive? (Shifting your breathing from chest to abdomen will in itself quiet your body down, if at the same time you can let your upper body relax. Practice this.)

• The next time you meet a stranger at a party, make it your aim to keep him or her talking about himself for fifteen minutes—without letting him realize that's what you're doing. Your job is to be so attentive and interested that he becomes completely absorbed in his subject (himself). Now what does that feel like? You had to remain quiet yet alert and responsive, and concentrate on someone else. Do you sense how rare this is for you? Do you begin to realize how pervasive your tendency is to stampede every occasion, every encounter? And do you see how much you're missing when you can't receive from others, can't hear what they're saying to you?

The point is not to become a passive person, but to give yourself more choices. Consciously developing the weaker side of your personality enables you to respond more flexibly and appropriately to the demands of any situation, broadening your range. And having more choices automatically makes you more sensitive to the moment, tells you when you ought to take charge, when you should sit back and watch and listen, when to give out and when to take in. You'll no longer be a single-gear bulldozer but a fully responsive human being.

Food: Eating Light

A lifetime fitness plan is imperative for endo mesos; you can very quickly burgeon into obesity if you let yourself go, and you're at the highest risk of any group for cardiovascular disease. You also have the greatest potential for a strong, powerful, beautifully muscled body. It's best if you take yourself in hand early, but it's never too late to gain or regain control. Follow the dieting program for endos and meso endos on pages 51–52 and 69–70. A few more tips that will help:

- To reduce your intake of saturated animal fats (which are the main dietary culprit in cardiovascular disease), learn to use meat as flavoring, with most of the volume coming from vegetable sources. For example:

  Chef's salad: thin strips of beef, chicken, ham, and cheese mixed with lots of lettuce, cucumber, green pepper— whatever greens you like—and a dressing with a low-fat yogurt base.

  Burrito: A cornmeal tortilla wrapped around a mixture of beans and salsa, with a little ground chicken or beef or cheese.

  Red beans and rice: Just that, flavored with little bits of smoked ham.

- Substitute spice for fat. The same principle of cheating your taste buds. Season your food as the Indians and Mexicans do; they also use meat as a minor ingredient in dishes that are mainly vegetables or grains. Oriental and Mediterranean cuisines make sophisticated use of spices along a gamut that ranges from delicate and subtle to fiery.

- High-fiber foods are not only good for the digestive tract, a diet that is high in fiber is automatically lower in fat. Some fiber even lowers cholesterol by itself, especially oats and oat bran—and oats also bind sugars; some diabetics have been able to go off insulin when put on a diet featuring oats. The top fiber foods: dried legumes (see the chart on page 70 for ways of combining them with other vegetable sources to give you complete protein), bran, fresh peas, lima and green beans, corn, whole-grain cereals, potatoes (including skin), broccoli, brussels sprouts, carrots; raspberries, blackberries, strawberries, cherries, plums, pears, bananas, and apples.

Our national diet has been so high in fat for so long that most of us associate a good meal with a heavy sensation in the stomach afterward—which comes from the fat. But this is a learned reaction, and one that disappears after the ratio of fats to carbohydrates has been reversed. At first you'll feel hungry too quickly after a meal, but once you become accustomed to eating "lighter," you'll prefer it. You can feel "full" with carbohydrate volume, without fat-soaked satiation.

Exercise: Getting Strong

In exercise for endo mesos, aerobics come first, not only for their cardiovascular benefits, but also because they raise the metabolism (as much as 25 percent), burn off fat, lower blood pressure, reduce the danger of blood clots, help control diabetes, reduce the risk of some cancers, such as colon cancer, and—perhaps most important of all—make it much easier to stay on a diet. Endo mesos who successfully control their weight are the ones who combine diet with aerobic exercise.

- The aerobics you'll find best suited to your body type and therefore easiest to maintain are swimming, cross-country skiing, cycling, and walking. Running you'll probably find an ordeal and won't keep up.

- Another sport that takes advantage of your low center of gravity and confers great aerobic benefit is karate. Once you're in training and can perform it for at least twenty minutes at a stretch, it burns calories at a rate equal to running and cross-country skiing, and done properly results in remarkably few injuries (fewer than most runners sustain). But in this sport, finding the right teacher is vital. Be sure yours is in good shape himself, and watch a class to see how you like the other students' work.

- An increasingly popular team sport that conditions aerobically much more effectively than football or even tennis is soccer.

• Aerobics burn off fat, and weight training builds muscle. Both men and women can benefit from weight training: Endo meso men can build impressive muscle mass; endo meso women can develop firmness, definition, and strength (even in the same body-type group, there are still sex differences). Here is a weight workout program for both sexes that gives you the most results with the least expenditure of effort:*

	Mon. Thu.	Tue.	Wed. Sat.	Fri.
Squat		X	X	X
Stiff-leg deadlift		X	X	X
Regular deadlift		X	X	X
Crunch		X		X
Lat pulldown	X		X	
Curl	X		X	
Bent rowing	X		X	
Shrug	X		X	X
Upright rowing	X	X	X	
Bench press	X	X		X
Behind neck press	X	X		X
Press	X	X		X

You can use a barbell and barbell plates, adjustable dumbbells, or the increasingly common home machines. The exercises are illustrated in innumerable books now on the market; among the best are *Bodybuilding: A Scientific Approach*, by Frederick Hatfield (Chicago: Contemporary Books, 1984); *The Gold's Gym Training Encyclopedia*, by Peter Grymkowski et al. (Chicago: Contemporary Books, 1984); *Arnold's Bodybuilding for Men*, by Arnold Schwarzenegger (with Bill Dobbins) (New York: Simon & Schuster, 1981); and *Pumping Up:*

---

*"The Ultimately Efficient Workout: Maximum Results with Minimum Effort" was developed by Professor Steven Goldberg for *Powerlifting USA* magazine. I am grateful for Professor Goldberg's permission to use it here.

Supershaping the Feminine Physique, by Ben Weider and Robert Kennedy (New York: Sterling Books, 1985).

Every exercise (except for the curl, included because everybody wants a special biceps exercise) works a number of muscle groups, not an individual muscle; this gives you the best return for your investment in time and effort. The whole routine takes about half an hour a day. For each exercise, proceed as follows:

• Find a weight that permits you to do the movement eight times, but not nine; you fail on the ninth. Say that for the squat it's 100 pounds. Your first set of the exercise will consist of eight squats, using 100 pounds (100 × 8). Now find a (lower) weight that again permits you to do eight reps (repetitions) of squats, and fail on the ninth. Say, 70 pounds (70 × 8). Now find a (still lower) weight (say, 50) that permits you to do fifteen squats and fail on the sixteenth. You have now done three sets, of eight, eight, and fifteen squats respectively. (It may take time to work up to three.)

Using that same series of weights (100, 70, and 50 pounds), work following the schedule on page 126 until you can do twelve reps on the first and second set, and twenty on the third. In the workout following the one on which you reach that number of reps, add sufficient weight (say, 5 pounds) to return the number of reps you can do per set to the original number: eight, eight, and fifteen.

It may take some experimenting before you find the right beginning weight for each exercise. But follow this plan regardless of how much or how little weight you can lift; some women may not be able to lift more than the barbell itself at first.

• If you don't want to build muscle mass (most women don't; most men do), increase not the weight but the number of reps at the same weight, doing all three sets at higher reps: twelve, twelve, and twenty times, respectively. This will emphasize endurance over one-time lifting strength.

- Never end a set simply because you've reached a certain number of reps; always work to the point where you try to lift the weight and can't. It's the last increment of effort that makes all the difference.

- Be sure to lift weights *smoothly*. Don't stop at the top or the bottom of the movement; always go through the entire range of motion each time. (This will maintain flexibility and prevent your getting muscle-bound.)

- *Keep breathing*. Exhale on the lift, inhale between movements.

- Rest no more than a minute or two between sets. If you need to rest longer, do so between exercises, not between sets of the same exercise.

6. ECTO MESOS: Lean and Taut

Who You Are

You're the swift predators, the loners, the prowlers and hunters. In you, meso drive is dominant, with ecto inhibition and restraint at secondary strength. You're complex people, often difficult, never dull. More frequently than any other group, you're to be found at the extremes of both good and evil.

What complicates you is that not only are you low in the endo component of relaxation, whose absence always imparts a chill, but your dominant meso drive also has to force its way through a restricting ecto. Your drive is intensified by your ecto narrowing of the channels of expression, so that it emerges only against resistance, and with concentrated force—and is iced besides, by lack of endo.

You may be effervescent, bubbling with gaiety but with the tingle and sting of dry champagne; you may be prickly and abrasive; you may sparkle with frost; or you may be all these things while suggesting the darkest depths. But however the ingredients combine, you ecto mesos are never warm, wet, or gushing; you're always spare, dry, cool.

It's easier in a way to define you by what you are not, by your dislikes and denials, than by what you actively are and desire. You despise every form of excess. You're the enemy of thickness, softness, slowness, complacency, of whatever is cozy and content. You resist accumulation—of possessions, of people. You travel alone and light, continually shedding all but minimal baggage. You have few attachments; you're efficient and merciless, and when you're finished with a lover, the amputation is surgical in its finality. No lingering tenderness or regret, just a quick, clean cut.

You feel a natural affinity with all wild things, with whatever can't be brought under the domestic yoke. In you the social impulse burns low; you're always asking embarrassing questions, as though you had no instinctive feeling for how other people "work"—and prove your lack of understanding by behaving as if you can find out by interrogation:

"How come a pretty girl like you never got married?"

"Aren't you sorry you never had a son?"

"You must have gained forty pounds since I saw you last. How could you let yourself go like that?"

Or even: "How did a guy like you ever manage to get so far? It must be some kind of knack that has nothing to do with brains."

And all in a tone of frank curiosity, without the least intention—consciously, at any rate—of giving offense.

No social gestures come easily to you, but you have great charm when you want to use it. You're superlative listeners; if someone interests you (but that's a big *if*), you'll zero in on him or her with a flattering concentration that excludes everyone but the two of you. And you'll remember what he said, too: He's registered; he exists for you, and more deeply than he would in the memory of a more superficially affable endo. At the same time, though, if you're socially ambitious your lack of innate warmth can make you somewhat calculating. You're not naturally gracious, so you feel you have to work at it. "I've got to learn to smile with my eyes; they're too cold," you'll admonish yourself in your journal; or, "Put more inflection in your voice, and talk slower; you sounded like a machine gun on that tape."

But these self-taught mannerisms rarely fit you comfortably, or become unconscious habit. On the contrary, as you grow older you become increasingly aware of the distance between what you feel and what you hope you're expressing, and you're more ill at ease with others than ever. For you're the cat that walks by itself, and you lack the instinct for making yourself popular. You're most acutely uncomfortable as a raw adolescent, before you've acquired grown-up social skills, but later in life you may become even more detached and coldly judging. Ecto mesos are often very handsome people, slim and clean-cut, but as a friend of one remarked, "He was as beautiful as an angel—a pitiless bright angel with a sword." You have a certain dramatic power, of the sort possessed by self-conscious people who are also sharply intelligent, and you can be highly, if cruelly, entertaining. But you also know when to withdraw silently into the background, to listen and absorb—and store up ammunition for later.

Even when you're not being deliberately cruel, you can be supremely tactless; you have little respect for social convention, and none at all for the minor hypocrisies and white lies that oil the machine. You cut to the bone. But you are even tougher on yourself than on others, are your own most merciless judge. Fooled by nothing and nobody, a part of you is always coolly surveying your own life from an ironic distance. Even in calamity, you're never so immersed that you can't offer a wry comment upon it.

Like Julian, who against his better judgment became engaged to Jessie. It seemed like a good idea at the time—at least it made her happy—but as the wedding drew near, he increasingly felt that the whole thing was all wrong. He could hardly bear to look at Jessie's excited face, rosy from shopping and fittings and showers, and he became more and more despondent. "The trouble with being engaged," he told his best friend, "is that you don't yet know the girl well enough to say to her that getting married is going to be a terrible mistake."

Too soon it was the night of the bachelor party. There was some desperate drinking, especially by Julian, and an ugly scene, and then a fight. No one knows quite what happened, but suddenly somebody was brandishing a gun, and Julian and another man were shot—the other with a grazing wound in the upper arm, Julian in the chest, fatally. As he was being carried out on a stretcher, he grinned and murmured to his friend, "You'll never believe it, but this was one way out I never thought of."

The Despotic Rule of Reason

Most people are stirred to action by some sort of emotion; the motor driving you ecto mesos, however, is more likely to be the force of an ideal or principle. Like all mesos, you're impelled by a will to power, but it's the idea that mobilizes your will. Whether you're a tyrant or a hero, a monster or a saint depends far more upon the kind of principle propelling you than the quality of your feelings. And once you're seized by an idea, you can be relentless in pursuing it; kindness, compassion, or fellow feeling is rarely strong in you. It's useless to try to convert you to a new view of things by moving your heart; the only way is to change your mind.

This is why you encompass, as few others can, the entire range of human aspirations, from one end to the other; it all depends on your idea, whether it's white supremacy or the brotherhood of man, rooting the Commies out of government or Liberty and Union, dissidents to the gulag or rocketing to the stars.

Emotionalism tends to temper the character; people who are guided by their feelings are rarely extremists, at either end of the scale. While they're not likely to be heroes or martyrs (and they may be killers), they're not absolutists, nor the ruthless autocrats that you cold reasoners can so easily become—and for all their potential for violence, they usually do less harm. Most people who reach high political office have the gift of emotional appeal; it's uncommon to find you dry rationalists at the pinnacle of power. Yet one of you became the greatest American statesman of them all: Abraham Lincoln.

"His reason ruled despotically all other faculties and qualities of his mind; his conscience and his heart were ruled by it," wrote Lincoln's Springfield law partner, William Herndon. "I know that it is generally believed that Mr. Lincoln's heart, his love and kindness, his tenderness, his mercy and his benevolence, were his ruling qualities, but this opinion is entirely erroneous in every particular. . . . He was not impulsive, fanciful, or imaginative, but cold, calm, precise, and exact. . . . He was a worshiper of principles and laws. To him everything was Law."

Ecto mesos are highly secretive, especially about motives. You meditate deeply before every important move; your plans have a long germination and gestation time. You can act very quickly, but it's never impulsive, in a release of feeling; your reflexive response may be rapid, but the motive force comes from deep inside you and is deliberate, never hasty or unthinking. Never do you tell anybody everything; whoever believes himself your confidant is self-deceived. No one knows you; your innermost self is always hidden.

Said Herndon of Lincoln: "He was a man of quite infinite silences and was thoroughly and deeply secretive, uncommunicative, and close-minded as to his plans, wishes, hopes, and fears . . . trusting no man, nor woman, nor child with the inner secrets of his ambitious soul. . . . He had his burning and his consuming ambitions, but he kept his secrets and opened not."

Lost Illusions

You are often torn by conflict. Your ecto whispers doubts, counsels caution even as your dominant meso impels you forward. This psychological dividedness can manifest itself in a variety of ways, but one of the commonest is an almost tragic awareness, even in the most dynamic and success-bound among you, of the gulf between appearance and reality, between surface brightness and what you perceive as inner corruption. It's ecto meso men, for instance, who are the most unrealistic about women, hurtling between adoration and loathing, idealizing them as goddesses, but the worship threatening to turn to hate if the woman refuses to stand still on the pedestal.

And it's you who, having scaled the heights, are plagued by those troubling questions that never occur to other mesos: "Is the game worth the candle, or is it all a fake and a delusion? What have I been working for? Have I been duped by the American Dream?" But even as you question the ultimate value of all you've striven for, you're just as tormented by dread of losing what you've got. You can never draw upon that deep confidence and trust, that inborn sense of security that endos possess like money in the bank. You're forever pondering not only "Is it worth it?" but also "Do I really have it?"

Transience is anguish. "One day you're king, a beggar the next." Where endo mesos enjoy these contrasts, riding life in all its colors just as it comes, accepting all, relishing all, you're likely to see even the golden promise as already tarnished, a worm at the heart of fulfillment. You're always staring at the skull beneath the skin: "In ten years my beauty will be gone." "I'm writing myself out." "We're way overextended; the crash is coming any day now."

You're driven by a vision—of glory, riches, fame, power and freedom (both at once); you want desperately to have it all. At the same time, though, you often can't succeed in thrusting away the darkening suspicion that your dream is either a hollow impossibility or a cheat, that the power has been bought at the price of freedom and self-respect.

Drinking helps to suppress these suspicions. A great many, perhaps most, alcoholics are ecto mesos. Drinking dulls the edge of conflict, loosens the cords of tension, allows the dominant meso to pull free, momentarily, from the inhibiting drag of ecto. And it also blunts the awareness of decay and loss. Baudelaire said of Edgar Allan Poe that he drank "barbarously, with . . . speed and dispatch as if he were performing a homicidal function, as if he had to kill something inside himself." The lost illusion may take the form of an ideal that proves false, or a love that betrays. You're sensitive to betrayal, see it on all sides; it justifies the quick, cool way you move in and out of the lives of others—whose complaints of betrayal are more legitimate than yours. But you never concede the right of anyone to confine you in any way. Even the women among you never cling, can never be held against their will.

Rebel Perfectionist

From earliest childhood Claire was always giving her mother the slip, streaking out of the house as fast and agile as a little cat. She was a daredevil tomboy, a reckless climber and diver and showoff.

Until adolescence she was stronger and better coordinated than any of the boys in her gang, and secretly believed that growing up meant becoming a boy. And when the other girls began clustering in giggling flocks, exploding in little shrieks as the boys hovered near, Claire turned surly and defiant. She still ran around with the boys she'd always known, but she refused to play the sexual game with the older ones. Like the other girls she could feel her body blooming, but to her it was a defeat, not a fulfillment.

Unmanageable before, she now became known as wild, stopping at nothing, kicking against all restraints, even the bonds of gang loyalty. All she needed was to hear that a thing was forbidden or impossible, and she would rush out and do it or taunt someone else into risking it. There were a couple of incidents within a few months of each other, one in which a girl was badly hurt and another in which a boy was killed. Her family succeeded in hushing them up, but after that Claire was shunned as "mad, bad, and dangerous to know."

She had a talent for drawing, so after high school her family, mainly to get rid of her, sent her to the Chicago Art Institute, where she studied with Frederick Benson, one of the great figures of American modernism. A gifted teacher, Benson recognized Claire's gift and under his demanding guidance she learned discipline at last. But at the end of the year she bolted, without finishing the course, in rebellion against her own temptation to let him influence her, become her mentor.

She went to Europe, and for months no one heard from her or of her. Then she surfaced, surprisingly, in the Paris atelier of Mme. Vrais, the great eighty-year-old classicist of haute couture. Mme. Vrais's clothes were as pure and beautiful—and as similar—each season as they had been for the past fifty years. In fact, the actual fifty-year-old dresses looked better than the new ones made by most of Mme. Vrais's competitors.

No question of a mentor there; Mme. Vrais barely acknowledged Claire's presence in the workroom, spoke to her seldom, sat alone most of the time in her bare white cell, hunched over her sketchboard puffing cigarettes. But after four years she allowed Claire to cut a couple of the muslins, and after six years a few of Claire's own designs appeared in the collection. When Mme. Vrais died, her syndicate of backers offered the succession of Maison Vrais to Claire. But by now she was restless again and wanted to go back home. She'd learned how to make clothes; now she needed to learn how to sell them.

Today Claire heads her own Seventh Avenue empire, a classic in her own right, famous for her cleanness of line, her cutting away of all superfluous "fat," of anything merely decorative. The spirit of unruliness as a girl, Claire at last found her "voice," as *Vogue* calls it, in the most severe geometry, as though she'd discovered that in this rigorous discipline of form lay some ultimate freedom. She celebrates the female body not as a sensual object, yielding and pleasure-giving, but as a Winged Victory, a prow cutting through air. "Clothes as architecture!" cried *Vogue*. "An American Original, a Formalist of Fashion!"

From a wild and headstrong teenager, Claire has metamorphosed into a dedicated workaholic. She's famous as a difficult, exacting employer, a perfectionist who offers no words of praise when a thing is right, who speaks to underlings, icily, only when she's pounced on a flaw. "But when you come out of her shop, you really know how to cut fabric," her ex-apprentices say. "And wherever you go from her, you can name your own price."

She has never married, probably never will. What she tells her friends is that the idea of waking up next to the same man day after day is too boring to contemplate, and a series of different men is too much trouble. The truth is that to Claire (and to the kind of men who attract her) sex is a contest of wills—a struggle both for dominance and self-sovereignty. She's had a few intense love affairs, which she has kept deeply secret, one in Paris, another in New York, breathless battles that locked the two of them in a death grip, unable either to surrender or break free, the impasse resolved at last only by exhaustion.

Vision of Devastation

Ecto mesos have great strength but not much elasticity. You tend to be rigid, brittle; you break, but you don't bend. Sometimes you become charismatic leaders, but your rise to power owes nothing to any skill at playing the political game. You lack all instinct for conciliation and compromise, the sense of when to stand fast and when to yield, when to hold the line and when to start bargaining. To you every issue is an absolute; it's as though you don't know any other way to act except all-out.

"It was a revelation," a one-time associate will recall, "to realize that what for me was a trivial matter of a few points more or less, a bit of give and take, was for Ralph a to-the-wall duel to the death. It was quite an experience to stroll innocently into his office one morning for a little talk about some minor policy question, and almost before I could blink, see the cords on his neck pulsing like ropes about to break and his whole body literally shaking with fury. I never saw anybody move so fast from neutral to killer rage. But he got like that a half a dozen times a day. And he never really let go in between—I guess there *was* no in-between. He was either quite wired or totally wired."

Nor do you ecto mesos often make successful administrators or executives, if that means carrying other people willingly along with you in achieving your aims; you're likely to get the job done at the cost of alienating everyone around you—including, in the end, even your own yes-men. John

Silber, the president of Boston University, has spent fifteen stormy years subduing a vociferous opposition among his faculty, who have frequently mutinied and at least once contemplated murder.

A typical Silber exchange occurred not long after he took office, when he spoke to the student body and afterward asked for questions from the floor. As reported by Nora Ephron in *Esquire* magazine, a boy rose from the audience with the polite complaint that the students felt "isolated from the administration." Silber answered, "You *are* isolated. Anybody who has read Kierkegaard knows that. And as you grow older, you will become more isolated. And when you die, you will be *all alone*. No one will be with you."

Not all of you harbor such a bleak outlook, of course, and if you do, you don't necessarily try to inflict it upon others. But most of you do exhibit a concentrated intensity of purpose and desire, like burning ice, that makes a lasting impression. A love affair especially leaves permanent scars. Maybe you'll escape clean and clear, but the other will never quite get over it.

"A Space to Think In"

In you ecto mesos, for every impulse there seems to be a contrary one, as though you're divided between your urge toward freedom, toward flight, and an equally insistent need to take control and dominate. You're shy and wild, but you also crave recognition—even while resenting your own longing for it. Ecto meso women have the hardest time because your need for appreciation and affection on the one hand, and for total independence on the other, are so difficult to reconcile. All of you experience some tension between your fundamental meso drive and an inhibiting ecto restraint, and you often resolve it by a determined stripping away of inessentials down to the clean, bare bones. You're impatient with excess in all its forms, whether emotional or aesthetic, detesting equally the overdecorated and florid in art or houses, and gushing and sentimental people. Stern, austere, hard on yourself and others, you seem continually impelled toward further purification and refinement, as though only by paring down to the essence can you finally arrive at the truth.

The painter Georgia O'Keeffe believed this, and exemplified it in the seamless unity of her work and her life. Strong and fiercely private, she was also determined to "make New York sit up and take notice" of her as the only serious woman artist in the circle around Alfred Stieglitz in the 1920s. O'Keeffe's love affair and reluctant marriage with Stieglitz is one of the romantic legends of American art, but she steadfastly refused to allow it to be written about and authorized no biography, no penetration of her privacy. She did however say this much about it: "Of course, you do your best to destroy each other without knowing it—some people do it knowingly and some do it unknowingly." And "there was a constant grinding like the ocean. It was as if something hot, dark, and destructive was hitched to the highest, brightest star."

Throughout her life she "took hold of anything that came along that I wanted." Traveling in New Mexico in 1934, she found and fell in love with an adobe ranch in a valley. "As soon as I saw it, I knew I must have it. I can't understand people who want something badly but don't grab for it. I grabbed."

In this dry, lonely place she lived sparely. "I like to have things as sparse as possible. If you have an empty wall you can think on it better. I like a space to think in. . . ." Her few furnishings included a glass-topped table that appealed to her because "it looks as though it almost didn't exist."

Out here, alone, she continued her fascinated study of the pure forms of nature, "shapes that were clear in my mind." To her a rock or a bone was no inert, dead thing; she painted animal skeletons because "the bones seem to cut sharply to the center of something that is keenly alive on the desert, even though it is vast and empty and untouchable—and knows no kindness with all its beauty."

Ten years ago she said, "I have never cared about what others were doing in art, or what they thought of my own paintings. Why should I care? I found my inspirations and painted them." In her late nineties she became almost blind. Her response was to find a new artistic life, as a sculptor. And here, too, as always, she followed none but her own inner light.

Well-being for Ecto Mesos

Letting Go

In ecto mesos the clash between meso and ecto can result in an overbearing, intolerant personality that tries to impose its views on others almost by force. Your contentiousness makes you difficult to get along with, but you're no easier on yourself; the internal conflict, often expressed as anger, you frequently take out on yourself in the form of alcoholism. You have great energy, but it's uneven in its delivery, jerky, spasmodic. You're also likely to suffer from stress-related ailments: exhaustion *and* insomnia (both), tension headaches, ulcers.

All of which points unmistakably in one direction: You need to increase, in every way possible, the influence of endo in your body and your life. Endo brings ease, elasticity, warmth; relaxes and softens the permanently contracted muscles; slows and steadies the energy flow, makes it more reliably available to you.

While you're young, in your twenties and early thirties, the damage from the ecto-meso conflict isn't so apparent, although the erratic quality of your energy, your jagged ups and downs, are noticeable from the beginning. Tennis is your game, and lack of control your greatest problem; you're too often beaten by inferior players because your range is limited to the high intense end of the scale. You've got power and speed to burn, but little ease or flexibility, and therefore little control.

And this applies to every area of your life; it's almost impossible for you to let go. As you get older you tend to lose what little elasticity you had, moving within an increasingly narrow range of choices and often becoming dry, tight, and rigid. Even if this has already begun to happen, however, it's never too late to develop those missing traits, to learn how to slow down, relax, develop ease and repose. With you it's best to start with the body, that undeniable fact that may already be causing you some discomfort.

The first exercise:

• Unclench your jaw. It's safe to say "*unclench*," because it's virtually certain that you keep your jaw permanently locked—so tight, and so permanently, that the muscle is probably anesthetized and you can't feel anything there at all. It's the muscle that twitches in the face of the strong, silent movie cowboy who has reached the boiling point inside, and is thus eloquently expressive—you ecto mesos carry around a lot of explosive anger that's held in hard in that clenched jaw. But you won't explode if you let go. The gradual release of tension is like slowly letting off the steam in a pressure cooker—it's not dangerous, to you or anyone else. More dangerous is to continue letting the pressure build up inside.

The first step is to become aware of the tension and then, slowly and gently, not yanking impatiently, release it. Place a finger in the little hollow just in front of your ear and open and close your jaw. That movement you feel is the jaw hinge, and that's the point where you want to release. Now take your finger away and put your mind in that spot, and *without moving* your jaw, let it relax. Let it go . . . don't waggle it back and forth. Do you feel that in your effort to let it go you're clenching it still tighter? Then what *do* you do to let it relax? Nothing—and that's the hard part. You're so used to associating every effect with making some movement, that not to move (that is, not to contract some muscle) is scarcely within the range of your kinesthetic imagination. (The kinesthetic sense is your sense of your own muscles.)

Now send your mind into your jaw hinge and think "release . . . soften." Not that "you" release "it," but that it releases itself. Persist with the thought of release—gently, patiently; it's a lifelong habit you're undoing. Since the tightening pulls the jaw back toward the ears, letting go will feel as though it's softening forward. But don't *push* it forward. *Think* the jaw soft, floating—feel your whole face softening. It may feel strange at first, empty, a nothing; the release of cramped muscles can be momentarily disconcerting. You'll know you've succeeded in freeing your jaw when you feel yourself salivating (this is a temporary effect). Nor does letting go of your jaw mean you have to walk around with your mouth open; you've got antigravity reflexes that keep it closed even when your jaw is relaxed.

This will be a new kinesthetic experience for you, and it's a crucial one, for the jaw tension is transmitted down through your neck and shoulders into your back, ultimately creating tension all the way down your spine to the base, into and even beyond the pelvic area—so that letting go of your jaw, once you've mastered it, releases tension in a reflex wave all the way down into your legs.

- Another focal point of tightness that is easier to sense and release is in the hands; you're continually clenching your fists. Think of your arm, from shoulder to fingers, as a garden hose; let the energy stream down like water, flowing all the way down from your neck out through the ends of your fingers.

If you practice this image at the same time that you let your jaw relax, you'll feel a new ease opening up and expanding through your whole body.

In the second exercise you go further inside yourself. It combines a form of meditation with conscious physical release, eases away deeper and deeper layers of tension, but you're always in control of the process because it happens through breathing.

- Lie down comfortably on the floor on your back, your head resting on a book two or three inches high, your arms and legs relaxed, slightly apart, not touching your body, and your mouth slightly open. As you lie there, simply become aware of the breath entering and leaving your body. Don't try to control it or change it in any way; just pay attention to it; follow its movement with your mind. And don't try to fill up, to pull the breath all the way into your upper chest (which is where you're usually aware of your breathing).

Notice how if you leave it alone, not pushing it out or pulling it in, the breath moves in and out very freely. It will be a very small movement, scarcely more than a tiny pulse, since you're making no demand on it other than to keep you alive as you lie there. Notice especially that if, when you've reached the end of your exhale, you simply pause and wait, the breath moves back in by itself. All you need to do is wait.

Now start to become aware of any tensions in your body that might be interfering with the freedom of the breath—particularly in the stomach and pelvic floor muscles. Can you feel what *tight-assed* means? Can you let go of the grip on your buttocks? Are you clenching your stomach? Can you let go of it? Think of the breath moving into these areas, washing away the tension as it ebbs out, flows in. Do you feel that you're holding anywhere else? In your rib cage? Your lower back? The backs of your thighs? Your hips? Move your mind lightly around your body and see if any of these places might want to let go a little more, as you continue to follow the movement of your breath flowing in and out of your body.

Now—still without doing anything—just think of the breath's movement as a double release: You're releasing to let it drop in, and you're releasing to let it drop out. On each movement of the breath, think of letting go a little more in your belly and buttocks. Imagine that your breath is dropping in and falling out of a hole in your belly.

Lie there for a few minutes and enjoy the feeling of release each time your breath moves in and out of your body. As you continue to think of letting go, as you release deeper and deeper, you may find your breath shifting gears, slowing down to a much deeper rhythm, in response to the relaxing of the abdominal and pelvic muscles. If so, just let that happen without interfering with it—it should feel very pleasurable, as though the letting go has opened up new places for your breath to flow into. You may feel breath dropping into your buttocks, your hips, as far down as your thighs. Let yourself have this new experience; enjoy it. Do you feel the easing in the very pit of your stomach? Do you feel your whole body becoming lighter, softer, warmer? Perhaps you feel nothing. Then "nothing" may be your experience of release—"something" being the tension of contracted muscles.

Explore your sensations; become acquainted with them. If you try doing this exercise every day for at least fifteen minutes—and it shouldn't feel like an "exercise" at all, only pure pleasure—you'll discover a whole new realm of peace and calm and comfort: inside yourself.

Food: Liquid Liabilities

You're the first group so far in whom endo is neither the dominant nor a secondary component. Wherever endo is low, weight control is rarely a problem; your spare, taut ecto meso bodies carry no excess weight, and you eat sparely in any case. On the contrary, you sometimes have trouble eating enough to maintain a weight sufficient for health. This is especially likely if you're a heavy drinker, for you're the type of drinker who doesn't eat, in whom the destructive effects of alcohol are enhanced by malnutrition. But even the nondrinkers among you are rarely enthusiastic about food; it's a boring necessity, never interesting in itself, as it is with virtually all endos.

• Avoid "empty calories," junk food that fills you up without nourishing you. You've got to make every calorie count, nutritionally. And alcohol itself is a form of junk food; it's got calories, but no food value. In addition, it depletes the body of the B-complex vitamins.

• If you drink, it's a good idea to take a daily multivitamin tablet, preferably one that emphasizes the B vitamins. Get one that has all the B's in equal strength. (The B vitamins are water-soluble, so whatever you take in excess of what your body can absorb washes out of your system. Their water-solubility is also the reason you need them every day.)

• You tend to be heavy meat-eaters, craving protein. As with all mesos, it's important that your animal protein be low in animal fat (except for saltwater fish; see page 106). Eat only limited amounts of eggs (no more than two a week), butter, and cheese.

- If you have one or more drinks before dinner, drink a glass or two of whole milk beforehand. This will coat the stomach, slow down the absorption of alcohol.

- Don't waste your calories on white bread. Eat only whole-grain bread; it's rich in B vitamins.

- A convenient, concentrated source of B vitamins is wheat germ. Sprinkle a tablespoon or two of it on your breakfast cereal.

- Or take a spoonful or two of brewer's yeast (from the health food store) in a glass of tomato or orange juice.

Exercise: It Breathes Me

- You're the most tightly muscled of any group; whatever sports you engage in, to prevent injury it's essential that you precede them with at least ten to fifteen minutes of stretches—slow, easy stretches to develop elasticity. *Never* bounce on the stretch, trying to push it further. Do it this way:

- From the initial position, move into the stretch *on* the outgoing breath until you come to the end of your elastic "give." Never force beyond that point. Stop as soon as you feel any resistance, and hold it there. Now continue releasing the breath out until you come to the end of it, release any tightness that may have taken hold, relax to let the breath drop in, relax to let it out, and just now, on that new outgoing release, let your body move a little further on the breath—if it wants to. It should feel as though the breath itself is moving you. Whether your body moves or not, continue releasing your breath and releasing your belly as you let the breath out. And come back to the starting position, and let the breath drop in.

    You'll find that if you confine your movement to the release in the direction of the stretch *on the breath*, your body will let go much more, whereas if you try to force the stretch, the muscle tightens up. This is the protective reaction of the "stretch reflex," which prevents a muscle from being pulled beyond a certain point. If you don't push, pull, or bounce, but think "release," you're freeing it for the maximum stretch possible.

• As you grow older, pay special attention to maintaining your body's flexibility—it's what you most quickly lose. If the sports you prefer emphasize speed and strength, such as tennis or squash, then balance them with another activity that encourages freer, more released movements, such as swimming, skating, or dancing.

III.
ECTOS:
The People of Mind

Ectos are long, slender,
sensitive, quick, and private.
Ectos come in three varieties:
balanced ectos, endo ectos, and meso ectos.

7. BALANCED ECTOS:
Slender and Delicate

Who You Are

In sensitive and high-strung balanced ectos, the ecto component is dominant, with endo and meso evenly balanced below. What sets you apart is your inherent complexity, which arises from a fundamental fact of your ecto organism: its sensitivity to all sensory stimuli, and its lack of enough endo or meso cushioning to absorb them comfortably. You're literally "thin-skinned"; your nerve endings are vulnerably close to the surface, which has little in the way of fat or muscle to fortify it.

You know yourself to be wary and apprehensive, your hyperextended antennae constantly on the alert for approaching danger. Your single most characteristic trait is your lack of complacency, of unthinking ease in the world. You're always watchful, always paying attention, rarely achieving unconsciousness. Even your sleep is light, restless, and full of dreams; your body may be at rest, but your mind never sleeps. Your most fervent—but unanswered—prayer is for relief from the relentlessness of awareness. Or at least that's what you *think* you want; but given the chance to surrender it—with alcohol or drugs, for instance—you'll put up a stiff resistance.

For you can't turn yourself into a bland, comfortable, accepting person, however much you'd like to; you may hanker after oblivion, but your sense of yourself depends upon your own ceaseless mental activity. A professor of particle physics at Columbia University once dropped in on one of those Human Be-Ins that were a feature of the 1970s. It took place in Riverside Park, near the university, and he was recognized by one of his students, who came up to him and asked, "How do you like what's going on, Professor Feinberg?"

"Well, it looks very interesting, and everyone seems to be having a good time, but I don't understand what they're doing."

"You're not *supposed* to understand, Professor. You're just supposed to do your thing."

"But understanding *is* my thing."

Freezing or Burnout

As the impressionable receivers of this world, you're exposed—often painfully so—to every kind of environmental stimulus, and you feel as if your circuitry is constantly in danger of burnout from overloading. To protect yourself, you resort to a variety of strategies of physical or psychic withdrawal, which in turn may prove a new source of danger—the danger of isolation.

Caught as you are between extremes, and naked to the world without the structural protection with which endos and mesos are endowed by nature, it's no wonder that you tend to be tense and nervous, wavering uneasily between the fear of invasion and of loneliness. You're fearful even of your own remoteness, perceiving yourself as fragile, brittle with the brittleness of glass, which can last forever if handled with care but, when it does break, shatters beyond repair.

Your dilemma was perfectly captured by Franz Kafka, a quintessential ecto, who told his fiancée, "I must be alone a great deal. What I accomplished was only the result of being alone"—but who also described himself, in his relations with others, as "a useless stake covered with snow and frost, fixed loosely and slantwise in a deeply plowed field on the edge of a great plain on a dark winter's night."

You'll be a panicky hypochondriac to the end of your long, healthy life—for you're singularly free from the degenerative diseases that afflict mesos and endos, and you're resistant to most infections. But it's you who become the health faddists, the cranks and eccentrics who seize on each new craze that comes along, forever seeking new ways of purging and purifying the "system."

The irony of you string-bean ectos who seem never to age, who haven't changed since high school, embracing one regime of spartan self-denial after another is almost too much for your endo friends to bear. "Don't tell me *you're* on a diet! For what, may I ask? That exact same plaid skirt you've got on now, safety pin and all, I remember you wearing twenty-five years ago in the ninth grade—and you haven't gained an ounce since then."

"Oh, it's new; it's the Acapulco Diet," you'll explain happily. "You can't have red food and white food at the same meal, and you can't have any fat or sugar at all."

Or no cooked food, or no raw food, or no protein and starch together; the point is the prohibition. Restraint always appeals to you—just the one who never needs to be told to cut down, who is always instinctively looking for new ways to simplify and prune the quantity of *stuff*—objects, people, events, emotions—you have to cope with, to process and absorb. Where endos and mesos can scarcely get enough of these things, you feel overburdened with them.

Endos and mesos are insatiable devourers of experience. They're avid for action, connection, acquisition. They want something happening all the time, can never get enough of anything. But you feel glutted and swamped by what you disdainfully regard as endo-meso excess. You always prefer quality to quantity, spareness to luxury, purity to profusion.

You're fastidious and discriminating. Experiences cut deeper with you, and you need more time to assimilate them.

You like houses with small rooms and low ceilings, bare walls, bare floors—and an attic and cellar. You prefer hard furniture, straight-backed chairs. What you really like is to be horizontal, with your feet higher than your head; your blood pressure tends to be low, and you feel best lying down. A characteristic posture is reclining on a sofa with your legs dangling over the back, or stretched out on the grass with your feet perched halfway up a tree.

Childhood Angst

You probably felt alien and somehow different from other people as early as babyhood. Often the first sign that your nature is going to be complicated appears with that perennial problem, eating. Ecto babies tend to be "underweight," often alarmingly so—underweight, that is, compared with endo and meso babies the same age. From the beginning, though, there's a remarkable contrast between the puny, skinny little body and its exceptional resistance to illness. But this goes along with an equal resistance to letting anything get inside without a lot of suspicious monitoring, and often the wholesale rejection of entire classes of foods.

Some ecto children seem to subsist exclusively on milk for their first ten years; others will eat nothing but peanut butter sandwiches or tuna fish. This extreme phase usually tapers off by puberty, when the terror of being conspicuous overtakes the fear of being poisoned. But still every forkful is scrutinized and interrogated before it's permitted to cross the frontier: "What are those horrible black specks? What's that stringy green stuff? What are those hard little lumps?"

And this same suspiciousness darkens and sharpens your other responses too. Not for you the joyous, thoughtless merging with or confronting the world that comes naturally to endos and mesos; you weigh and debate every impulse before acting upon it, and reject most of them. Young ecto children are usually to be found wistfully looking on at the doings of the others, missing nothing but seldom taking part. At the playground, where the meso children run things, ectos are the needle-eyed watchers on the sidelines.

A pattern emerges during childhood that will persist throughout life: It's equally painful and tragic for you to be invited to join in, and not to be invited. Either you're being forced into the action against your will or excluded from it, and both make you miserable. "There's simply no pleasing him," your exasperated parents complain. "He whines no matter what I do." But it's the same old dilemma. You're caught between two piercing vulnerabilities: In any activity you feel you can too easily get trampled, but you can freeze, too, in loneliness.

Ecto children are not cowards or sissies; on the contrary, you're braver than most, for it takes a conscious and determined effort of will to act when every action is a felt risk. For an ecto to expose his bony little body in a free-for-all or a football scrimmage or even worse, to exhibit his frail skeleton in swimming trunks, takes real courage—often the courage of desperation. You know all about both courage and despair, far more than those to whom bold, vigorous action comes naturally and unthinkingly.

Fortunately, you can console yourself with a vivid fantasy life, full of dreams of glory. In the imaginary world you can be everything that's impossible for you in this one: strong, confident, popular, king of the playing field. And this ability to dream is not just wish-fulfilling escapism. Several studies have shown that late-maturing ectos who are sustained by fantasy as children develop a better sense of humor as adults, a broader tolerance for ambiguity and the idiosyncrasies of others, and a livelier and more creative imagination.

But childhood, in the meantime, is full of anxiety and dread. Physically and emotionally you tend to lag behind endos and mesos, as though your organism were holding back, reluctant to take the plunge. Your developmental curve is slower, and you never feel capable of moving out into the world with any confidence. You're always being pushed to perform before you're ready; as Kafka lamented, "Still unborn and already compelled to walk around the streets and speak to people."

The period of the early adolescent growth spurt, never an easy time for anyone, is especially hard on ectos, who attain their maximum linearity during these few months. All gangly angles and awkwardness, what secondary endo you possess is in temporary abeyance, leaving you with even fewer resources than usual to protect and smooth the edges.

Late-Blooming Loner

Adolescence is especially hard on ecto girls. Someone has said that high school kids have the souls of petty bourgeois, and what truth there is in that remark certainly applies to their standards of beauty. In the whole history of high school, there's probably never been an ecto prom queen. You come into your own much later, in your twenties or thirties, when the scrawniness has softened into slenderness, the sharp corners gently curved by the reemergent endo, your long, slim legs admired by more sophisticated eyes. The prom queen, meanwhile, snatched up early into marriage, has probably thickened into a dumpy mother of four. But try telling that to an hysterical fifteen-year-old whom no one has asked to the prom at all.

Or—worse yet—who *has* been asked. Mimi's mother's best friend has a son who is a junior on the basketball team. His whole family has joined forces to press-gang him into sullen service this fragrant June night. Mimi is in a panic of expectancy and terror. When he comes to pick her up, what will they talk about? What if he doesn't even show up? What if he refuses to speak to her at all? If he does speak, what will she think of to say to him? What if he won't dance with her? What if he doesn't know how? What if he tries to kiss her? What if he doesn't?

For Mimi has never been alone with a boy before, never had a date. Even grown-ups are nervous around this bony waif with the eyes too big for her face. They sense in her a covert critic with a wicked gift for mimicking the ludicrous side of the powerful and intimidating. Like all vulnerable people, she's got a merciless eye for the buried sensitivities of others, and in her private theater of the ridiculous she skewers them.

But in a group she's defenseless and lost. She's the kid who brings a cherished pet horned toad as a birthday present, when what's expected is a charm bracelet; who hides in the bathroom when the other girls cluster around the telephone breathlessly calling up boys. Her mother tries to reassure her that she's just a "late bloomer," but the truth is she will never feel she's quite "got it," never feel at ease in the world. Life will always seem like a performance for which she hasn't yet learned her lines or acquired the right costume or mastered her stage business. The performance gets smoother as she gains experience, but she'll never lose the sense that it *is* a kind of act, that there's a distance between her "real" critical yet shrinking self and the self that nods and smiles and talks to people, that pretends to poise and grace.

Twenty years after that first prom, Mimi still feels threatened by an elevator ride in her own apartment building. It's a "situation": you're trapped inside with a neighbor you recognize but don't really know to speak to. What do you do? Do you say hello? What then? Is any further conversation required? If so, what kind? What manner should you adopt? Horror of eyes meeting—but where to look to avoid them? And to avoid appearing to avoid them? Do you pretend to be alone? Gaze into space? At the end of a journey from penthouse to street, Mimi emerges flustered, breathing a little faster from the strain. And having somehow created, with all that studied avoidance, an atmosphere freighted with sexual promise, or menace.

Covert Operations

Physically, too, you're tense and tight—not with the tension of flexed muscles poised to spring into action, but restrained, withheld. You walk with a "don't wake the baby" constraint at every step, a shrinking, retreating kind of tension, as though your body were trying to insulate itself from its own excesses of response, to escape from its own mind. Every gesture is a holding back rather than a giving forth; even your breathing tends to be shallow and inhibited.

Ecto faces are at once wary and mobile, full of nervous animation. You're alert and watchful, acutely aware of everyone and everything around you, while reluctant to reveal your reactions to them. You feel transparent, thinking everyone can see right through you. Your face has a look of strained attentiveness and a flickering aliveness that's very difficult to "read" for emotion—and in fact the emotions *are* both contradictory and held in. Your expression is neither open nor consistent. Your mouth is held tight, the lips compressed, and mouth and eyes may be saying quite different things, with both shifting in a flash. What you usually seem to be expressing is your own inescapable self-consciousness.

You have a strong, prickly sense of boundaries, and your greatest fear is of being encroached upon, of having your barriers breached. You hate to be touched; if someone puts a friendly hand on your arm you'll either twitch it away or freeze until it's removed. If someone lays a casual arm across your shoulders, your whole back bristles and arches. You're not a fondler or caresser; the only embrace you ever welcome is the sexual one, and then only at the orgasmic instant of self-forgetting.

You'll never willingly sleep in the same bed with anyone else, preferably not even in the same room. And you like to be covered up at all times; unlike your exhibitionistic endo and meso brothers and sisters, your favorite clothes are high-necked and long-sleeved, with deep pockets you can dig your fists into. You like hoods and broad-brimmed hats, shaggy sweaters, long skirts, baggy trousers.

Leap in the Dark

To you, truth is never to be found on the surface of things. What's visible is probably deceptive; an emotion expressed is most likely false. Anything that is sincerely felt lies too deep for show, you believe (in contrast with endos, for whom what doesn't show doesn't exist). You're fascinated by the hidden side of things, the buried truth; since surfaces are never satisfactory (starting with your own), you seek a reality beneath and beyond appearances.

You're the theoreticians, the dreamers, the prophets. The physical body, to begin with, is obviously inadequate, either as an explanation or an end in itself; you're all too conscious of how far your own body is from expressing what you consider important about yourself; and you go on from there to dismiss the whole sensual, physical world as full of lies and danger (again in contrast to endos, for whom it is the source of every good thing). To you, the material world is not only deceptive but scarcely manageable, always on the verge of overwhelming you, of exploding into anarchy and violence.

You're drawn to systems that promise escape from the chaos of appearances—what sort of system depending on the quality of your mind and experience. You may be a mathematician, a molecular biologist, or a philosopher. Or you may become a religious mystic, transcending the material body altogether, or a Zen Buddhist, or a spiritualist, taking flight into the Great Beyond. Or you may write or consume science fiction, constructing alternative worlds to this unpredictable and imperfect one. To you, God is the principle of Order in the universe. (To endos, God means Love and Beauty; to mesos, God is Power.)

But although you're likely to be a seeker after or a creator of systems, your actual thinking is usually anything but systematic. Your mind works in flashes; your ideas are born from the sudden sparking of disconnected images, but only after a long marination in the unconscious, a period in which nothing whatever seems to be happening—to the great anxiety of those whose livelihoods depend on the productivity of your mind.

You're always driving your endo and meso partners crazy with your irregular hours, your permanent air of disorder and confusion. You give the perpetual impression of having just arrived at, or beyond, the end of your tether: breathless, feverish, alternately stiff with tension and limp from exhaustion. Endos and mesos are methodical people, efficient, orderly in their habits, lovers of regular routines, of fixed schedules. With you, nothing ever becomes habitual or routine. You have no comfortable rituals, not even "good morning." Everything, even a simple greeting, has to be thought through fresh each time, and the only predictable element in your behavior is its unpredictability.

You usually do manage to deliver the goods, but only at the

eleventh hour and at a terrific cost in nervous wear and tear on yourself and everyone around you. You work in spurts. Your mind needs to dance around a problem, advancing and retreating, because you never know where the answer's going to come from; it's like a leap in the dark. While your circuitry is wired to get the maximum response from every input, most of that input proves useless; you can't help picking up on everything, and most of it is irrelevant. But that's the way you work, like it or not. You do well in partnership with endos or meso endos, who can exert a steadying influence, who prize your contribution but don't get pulled into your orbit of fluster and panic, who can impose some order in the form of firm schedules, a calm, reassuring environment.

Knives or Clouds

The sharpness of your sensations seems always on the verge of cutting you to pieces, like knives turned inward. A nervous breakdown feels always imminent, and one of your many paradoxes is your actual durability, a long life composed of a succession of just-about-to-be-intolerable moments.

You tend to be perceptive about the things that separate people, blind to those that unite them. You have an instinct for the unique, the isolated, have little sympathy with the commonplace, and you can alternate an acute, almost supernatural insight with the most obtuse ignorance. Your sympathies are always with the solitary individual, never with people in groups. You loathe such events as family reunions; you have a horror of gatherings to begin with, and one that brings you together with people in whom you can't help seeing yourself reflected as if in caricature is a nightmare. You're forever lamenting your loneliness and singularity, but would kill to maintain them.

Nothing that people do can surprise you much, or disconcert you. You expect life to be preposterous; never having developed any very fixed ideas of how things are "supposed" to be, you take the unexpected in stride. The discovery of a secret side to the character of someone you supposedly know well, the revelation that X has been stealing from the company all these years, or is a bigamist, or has been spying for Russia, never disconcerts his ecto friends, who take it for granted that things are not what they seem, for isn't this truest of all about themselves? The face you show the world is a makeshift, the best you can come up with for the moment, but in no way accurately represents what you "really" are. Like most aspects of your life, your social self is a temporary improvisation, not a permanent truth.

You slip back and forth easily between dreams and waking reality, for the dream world is wholly real to you, while the waking world often has the quality of a dream. And you sometimes wrap yourself in vagueness, becoming distracted, numb, as though deliberately severing the connection with the external world. You never seem able to mobilize a steady flow of energy or attention; your rhythms are fitful, uneven, and people can never tell whether in their approaches to you they'll be met with a stunning insight that cuts straight to the heart of the matter, or an impenetrable fog.

The Secret Self

Ectos can wreak havoc with the lives of people who don't understand that the social self you exhibit is not a self to which you feel any loyalty, but merely a convenient mask. Especially small, fragile ecto women, sexually charged, sexually vulnerable, and sexually irresistible to the type of man who is perhaps least well equipped to understand them.

A woman like Sara, married to Herbert, who says that after twelve years of living with her he still can't fathom in the slightest degree the way her mind works. Jittery, pessimistic— "Whenever the phone rings," she says, "I always wonder what I've done wrong, who's after me now?"—Sara is a chronic insomniac, a connoisseur of white noise whom no background music ever succeeds in lulling, whose mind is ceaselessly vigilant, but who seems, however, not to be too sure most of the time just where she is or whom she's with.

Compliant, trying hard to please, working like a field hand to become a good hostess for Herbert without possessing any of the instincts for it—and getting better at it, too; for the first few years of their married life, no meal was ever served with all its courses unscorched, intact, and in sequence, but she has since learned, laboriously, to cook, to set a table, to arrange flowers, even to chat with guests—Sara nevertheless, as Herbert is well aware, is ultimately loyal only to some complex and private set of values in which he cannot share, and which is finally incomprehensible to him.

When his father died last summer, for instance, a drawn-out death that began with a prolonged period of coma, it was Sara who insisted on keeping watch by his bedside. "Why don't you get some rest? He's in a coma; he can't possibly know you're there."

"How can you be so sure? Maybe he knows what's happening to him. Maybe it makes a difference to him to have someone here, so he's not alone. You go to bed if you want; I'm not leaving him."

And it was Sara who drove by herself to the crematorium at six in the morning, the day after the memorial service, to stay with his body until it was burned; almost bodiless Sara, acting out of an obscure impulse to accompany her father-in-law's worn-out body as far as she could on its longest journey.

But: "You think this is a woman whose kingdom is not of this world?" shouts Herbert. "You think what we've got here is some kind of a *saint*? Oh brother, do I have news for you!"

For Herbert has found out that Sara, in her somnambulistic way, has apparently gone to bed with most of his friends. Over the years, whenever he was away for a few days on a business trip, for a three-month period while he was setting up the branch office in Seattle, and most of the time in between, Sara didn't say no, it seems, to anyone who asked her.

"How could you do this to me?"

"It didn't matter, don't you see, Herbert, it didn't matter at all. None of them did, they just didn't count."

"What's that supposed to mean? Do *I* count, then? And what's the difference? What's the difference between Max, or Vernon, or Pete, or Bill, or Leonard, or Jack, and me, as far as you're concerned? *Is* there any?"

She is silent. Because he's right; for all his obtuseness, Herbert has got the point: that none of them, including him, has really mattered to her, has touched her in any deep way.

They were merely a succession of bodies. She's never had the least sense that she was betraying either him or herself or their marriage, at which she's worked so hard. Sara is equally faithful, and faithless, to them all, because none of them has had anything to do with her real self—which is precisely that part of her that none of them can ever reach.

Well-being for Balanced Ectos

Sound and Fury

Your well-being depends upon recognizing two facts that separate you balanced ectos from others: (1) the speed of your reactions; (2) the slenderness of your reserves of energy and endurance. The key word here is *reserves*. You've got as much energy as anyone, but it needs to be frequently replenished because you absorb and process everything you take in so rapidly. Hunger and fatigue hit suddenly, urgently, and often. You have a short metabolic cycle; you need to eat and rest much more frequently than endos or mesos do. More frequently—but not necessarily more. Both rest and meals can be brief and light, and soon you're ready to take off again.

The stress of excessive exposure to what ecto Jerry Brown calls "the sound and fury of an overstimulated world" often shows up first as troubled skin. Yours tends to be dry and susceptible to allergic reactions, itching, rashes, bruising, and blemishes. It needs more protection than endo or meso skins, especially in cold weather. When you're exercising out of doors in the winter, be sure to use a rich emollient cream before exposing your face to the wind, and as a daily practice apply oil or cream *over* a damp skin; this both locks in moisture and serves as a protective barrier.

Your skin sensitivity is part of your general pattern of physiological overresponse, the trigger-happy internal alarm system that activates the body's defenses at the slightest disturbance. It makes you hyperreactive, but it's also responsible for your resistance to disease and your rapid recovery whenever you do fall ill. You are, however, more susceptible than others to upper respiratory tract infections such as colds, bronchitis, and flu.

But your most common symptom of stress is digestive upset. When you're anxious or unhappy, you have trouble eating enough to keep your weight up, and you suffer frequently from nausea, constipation, and diarrhea. Headaches are another common symptom. If the stress is prolonged, you're the people most likely to develop gastric or duodenal ulcers.

The treatment for all of these problems is simple: *regular and frequent* meals, rest, and exercise.

Food: Burning It Off

Unlike endos and mesos, when it comes to eating you can be guided by your appetite; what you like will probably be what's best for you.

Your stomach is small, the gut thin-walled and irritable, your whole digestive apparatus sensitive and easily upset. You're often hungry, but you can't handle much food at any one time. What usually doesn't work with you is two or three "square" meals a day which overload your small capacity, or foods that are difficult to digest. You feel best with more frequent, smaller meals consisting of foods that are easily absorbed. Because your higher metabolic rate tends to burn food fast, the spacing of meals is especially important.

You're less vulnerable than endos and mesos to the diseases in which diet is thought to be an important risk factor, such as adult-onset diabetes, cardiovascular disease, and some forms of cancer. For ectos, high-cholesterol foods are less hazardous than they are for mesos and endos. Your main dietary problem, therefore, is keeping your weight and your energy up; concentrate on making the business of eating as enjoyable as possible, and don't worry about adhering too strictly to any particular diet, provided it's reasonably balanced. Ecto George Sheehan puts it succinctly: "(1) Eat foods that agree with you; (2) Avoid foods that disagree with you."

• The foods that best agree with your small stomach and short digestive tract are animal proteins and the more easily digested carbohydrates. Fiber should be eaten in moderation; you need a certain amount but nothing like as much as endos and mesos do. You'll get all the fiber you need from two or three servings a day of fresh fruit and vegetables. Don't let yourself be bullied by nutritional ideologues into having bran every morning for breakfast. It will only irritate an already sensitive gut.

• On the other hand, the "excess" of animal protein that is undesirable, even dangerous for mesos and endos is not excessive for you. You tend to crave protein, owing to your body's high ratio of surface area to mass. The protein you eat is immediately expended in energy radiating from the surface; in other words, you burn it off fast. But it's not the high-fat, high-cholesterol marbled steaks and pork chops that you choose anyway; you usually prefer low-fat chicken and fish.

• If it's difficult for you to maintain a minimum weight, the advice given earlier for endos holds true for you, but in reverse:

(1) Do not fill up with low- or no-calorie liquids before, with, or between meals. Make everything that goes in count, calorically. Try eggnogs, milkshakes, or thick soups if you find it easier to drink than to eat (many ectos do). If milk upsets your stomach, try yogurt; it's much more easily digested.

(2) Limit the amount you eat of nutritionally empty fiber or roughage. Most of your vegetables and fruits should be high-calorie, low-residue, easily absorbed: rice, potatoes, squash, pasta, bananas, apricots, avocados.

(3) Include in your snacks foods such as dried fruits and nuts which have a high concentration of calories in a small volume. Did you know, for instance, that one ounce of pecans—less than a handful—contains over 200 calories?

(4) Eat as often as you can. Your small stomach cannot handle big, heavy meals. Try dividing your intake among six or seven small meals spread throughout the day, including just before bedtime.

Exercise: Thinking on Your Feet

You're happiest at activities that (1) are noncompetitive; (2) involve little or no body contact; (3) can be pursued alone or with one or two others; (4) don't require intense surges of power. Walking, running, swimming, cycling, hiking, aerobic dancing, all of which fill this bill, also confer the greatest aerobic benefits, and aerobics are the most essential to overall health. Your low proportion of fat to muscle and bone makes you less buoyant in the water than endos are, and while you *can* swim, it's not an activity that comes naturally to you or one you often choose.

• What you're built for, with your long legs and high center of gravity, is walking. You can set your own pace; it demands no great output of energy at any one time but builds endurance gradually, without strain; it provides a gentle but continuous workout for the entire skeletal-muscular system; and it reduces tension more effectively than tranquilizers. By lightly massaging the intestines, it even relieves constipation.

Walking is a tonic against the particular fatigue that results from long stretches of sedentary mental work at which so many ectos spend their days. And walking is a wonderful stimulus to thought. Rhythmically moving the large leg muscles seems greatly to relieve the physical tensions so often associated with problem solving. Writers, philosophers, mathematicians—professional thinkers of every kind, from Bertrand Russell to Isaac Bashevis Singer—have always sworn by walking. They'll tell you that their best ideas come to them while they're on the move.

If you can walk four miles in an hour, you can achieve excellent aerobic fitness. A twenty-minute walk at lunchtime will both relax and invigorate you for the afternoon's work. And another walk in the evening is the perfect way to unwind.

- You become dehydrated easily; be sure to take in plenty of fluids when you're exercising, especially if you run. Always, before going out for a run, drink a glass or two of water.

- If you're a pipestem-boned ecto, you can benefit from the weight training program described on pages 126–128. To accumulate much muscle mass you would need heavier bones to anchor the muscles to, but you can acquire strength and definition if you follow the basic plan. For endurance, follow the variation that suggests higher reps with lower weights.

8. ENDO ECTOS: Willowy and Quivering

Who You Are

You endo ectos are the exotics, the hothouse orchids, the most vulnerable, yet among the showiest. With ecto length dominant, endo softness secondary, and the meso that gives structural strength the lowest of the three, you're the boneless wonders, tall and wobbly, shakily overextended into space. Long, sinuous, and pliant, you're the most physically unstable, and therefore insecure, with a tendency to sway dreamily through life.

You're master procrastinators. When it comes to putting things off, you sweep the field, waiting until the last minute is upon you, then launching into a despairing wail: "I've got twelve people coming for dinner in *one hour!*" "My plane is leaving in exactly forty-five minutes, and I can't find my passport, and *nothing* is even *ironed!*" "That mean old Miss Grody said she'd *fail* us if we didn't turn our papers in *tomorrow morning!*"

It's not that you expect *us* to do anything; not even God

could help you now. But of course we, instead of moaning, see what can conceivably, if we sacrifice our own evening, be done to save the situation, and we do it. Then it's "Oh, Barbara, you are *so* brilliant. Look, everybody, how be*yoo*tiful-ly Barbara has mended my jacket (typed my essay), (made the crust for the beef Wellington). Oh, Barbara, you are so lucky to be so talented!"

Says Barbara resignedly, "Edie is such a terrific *appreciator*, and such a waif; sometimes it feels as though I've spent my life taking her hems up and down for her, or sewing sequins on her costumes, or cleaning her kitchen after a party. Why do I do it? I don't know; anything to dry those pitiful tears, I guess. I may be great at putting together a beef Wellington, but Edie is second to none at getting people to do things for her."

Night-Flying Moths

Every move you improbable creatures make, from the way you stand and walk and use your hands to your most flamboyant excesses, has its source in a bone-deep insecurity. If your first priority is getting yourself protected, a close second is a need to be noticed and admired. These two drives often collide, the urge to conceal yourself and to show off both finding expression at the same time, to bizarre effect. You'll dart breathlessly into a room full of people as though pursued by demons, stare about in wild confusion, and as soon as all eyes are upon you, fly out again with little hysterical shrieks. You're in constant motion, always just arriving or just leaving, half hiding, half exposed, draped over the furniture or flung down among a heap of cushions.

Yet somehow you're always on the scene. You never miss a party or an opening, incessantly showing yourself in public, where, amid the bright lights, you exhibit your overwhelming shyness. Like Lily, known from childhood as "Flopsy," who's always writhing in an agony of embarrassed self-conscious-ness, whose friends will tell you, "I don't think I've ever actually seen Lily head-on; when I think of her, it's more like a glimpse caught out of the corner of my eye." Lily has an instinct for making sure you never get enough of her to be bored. She's an epigrammatic presence, a glance, a whisper. But she *is* a presence. Lily never fades into the background; for all her vaporousness, somehow you always notice her.

Often in the evenings she'll get a "teensy bit tiddly" (although she scarcely drinks at all, not *really*, never before evening, and only to overcome her paralyzing timidity). But she doesn't hold it terribly well—at least, she doesn't hold it inconspicuously. Many a night out with Lily finishes early, with her curly head under the table and her tiny satin-slippered feet waving helplessly in the air over the soup.

For someone who makes such a parade of defenselessness, she's oddly trusting; typically, one's last view of Lily is passed out, being carried off, her chiffon skirts and limp arms trailing the carpet, by some man she's just met that evening. Lily has awakened in some very strange beds in her time; but she always manages to find her way back to her usual haunts by evening, refreshed and ready for anything.

Like all ectos, you endo ectos gain strength as the day progresses. You're twilight and evening people, not only because your energy rises toward nightfall but also because you're sensitive to sunlight, and usually feel best when the light is dim, or at any rate artificial. You like to wear sunglasses at all times whenever you're outdoors, even in dead of winter, even at night.

Like all ectos, too, you dislike being touched, and you're so self-conscious that a gaze or even a glance is as intimate as a caress—or a blow. Looking at you is almost as intrusive as touching. Yet you need to be looked at in order to feel that you fully exist.

You're like plants with delicate, curving tendrils, clinging rather than free-standing. Your colors are the shades of twilight: mauve, peacock blue, olive, lavender, burnished gold, rose, lilac, vermilion, chartreuse. You prefer your lighting effects crepuscular, too: purplish shadows and discreet, softly shaded light, muted, "kind," illuminating you with gentleness and tact.

Life, as you anticipate it in your adolescent fantasies, is a drama in which the events are secondary to the lighting effects, the costumes, and the decor. It's a series of scenes in which you move gracefully about the stage in elegantly furnished rooms, lovingly lit, exquisitely dressed, the still center of the action that swirls about you. Your dilemma is to be caught between the need to be known and to remain private, screened from any indifferent or callous gaze. You want desperately to be seen and recognized, but only by the eye of unconditional love.

Wavering Wanderers

You conceive of life as far as possible in aesthetic terms. The key to most of your behavior is artifice; you see nature as an enemy, an alien and hostile force to be continually circumvented, outwitted, held at bay. You know yourself to be an exception, a kind of biological sport, and therefore endangered. Often you'll try to construct a hedge against a threatening reality by concentrating on acquiring or creating the "perfect"—black satin pants, arrangement of tuberoses and delphinium, dinner party, sonnet stanza. But you're ectos, after all, and like an ironic comment, some overlooked detail usually gives the game away: There's dust on the table holding the flowers; the main course is carbonized; the shoes beneath the pants are scuffed and stained.

You have a light touch in everything—light of hand, of heart, of wit—glancing, skimming. You're never ponderous or self-important; how could a jellyfish give itself airs? One never hears from you the pomposities that mesos are sometimes given to. But you're altogether lacking, too, in calm and self-possession. With little innate self-confidence, even when you know your own value you can see no way of imposing it upon the world. You just float, airily, precariously, and hope that you'll be appreciated as you drift by.

And just as you're both shrinkingly shy and longing for the limelight, you also crave simultaneously intimacy and solitude. You may suffer agonies of loneliness, but you're equally frightened of the ties and obligations of love. You reach out tremulously, tentatively, but take flight when anyone moves toward you. It's always best to let you make the approach, which will be apprehensive, wavering, advancing a step, then pulling back in alarm before venturing forward again. It takes a lot of patience and forbearance to achieve any degree of intimacy with you.

Once a friendship is formed, though, it's likely to last forever—not, however, thanks to any firmness on your part. You're notoriously unable to achieve what psychologists call "closure"; you dread bringing anything, however worn out, to an end, preferring to wander through life trailing behind you like damp seaweed the shreds of dead loves. Neither at the beginning nor the end of a romance can you ever say no, which lands you in some sticky messes that leave an aftermath of rancor.

An endo ecto girl being proposed to, or propositioned by, someone she doesn't love and never could love, first blushes and gasps, "Oh, I don't know . . . Oh, I really couldn't . . . Oh, I'm afraid I'd never manage . . ." Then (grasping at straws): "I can't ride, I could never keep up with you . . . I'm afraid of flying . . . I can't cook (that's it!), I'm a *terrible* cook, I can't even fry an egg, I live off frozen TV dinners, you'd starve . . . I'm disgustingly messy, I have to get someone to come in and clean before the cleaning woman comes . . . I'm allergic to dogs . . . I kick in my sleep."

When all these objections have been conquered by a stronger—and more obtuse—will than your own, you'll succumb for the moment, faintly agreeing to everything just so he'll go away. But it's a mistake to expect you to show up the next day at the airport, or at City Hall. Nor do you make reliable organization men or women; it's unwise to put you in charge of the catering, or of handling hotel accommodations for the visitors, or to ask you to serve on the steering committee. The result is likely to be huddled masses of wet, hungry, bedless, and furious guests charging about hunting for someone to blame. You neither refuse nor perform, but sort of fade away when the moment to deliver comes. What you're incapable of is simply saying, at the outset, "No, I don't want to," or "No, I won't," or even just "No." It's too . . . blunt, too final. Too definite. The haze of infinite possibility, in which no irrevocable steps are ever taken, nothing is ever foreclosed, is much more attractive.

You can be wildly jealous, but seldom for long, regardless of the provocation; your possessiveness is usually outweighed by a deeper need for solitude. It's common for you to be painfully, but perpetually, isolated; forever in dread of being alone, but somehow always in that condition, which you seem finally to prefer. Although you're intermittently excited at the notion of having a permanent witness to your life, someone to watch you as well as watch over you, who knows your feelings and doings as well as you do—at the same time the prospect is terrifying. From even the most sympathetic audience, you need frequent time off; the married among you prefer to sleep alone, spend your days away from the man or woman you live with, meet only in the evenings.

And the best way to bind you forever is to seduce and then desert you, brutally; you'll spend the rest of your days sighing and grieving for a lost paradise.

Sinister Shadows

Your reluctance to let go, to lose or finally give anything up, stems from a fear whose roots run as deep as your physical structure. You have a poor sense of process, lacking a feel for how things get done or made. To you it seems miraculous that a house can actually arise on that empty tract of land; that from a flat piece of rough leather a pair of shoes can emerge; that if one does certain things to flour, butter, and sugar, one gets a cake; that a glimmer of an idea can, after a sequence of actions, result in a magazine, a movie, a restaurant.

Your grasp of cause and effect can be feeble to an infantile degree. Unable to see that "if you do this, that will follow," or "if you want this, first you must do that," you're either terrified of losing everything at one blow, or alternatively can't understand why whatever you want shouldn't be instantly available. Everything you possess seems to have come to you by magic; even when you work for a salary, you don't fully realize that the check appears at the end of the week *because* you go to the office every day. The two facts aren't altogether connected in your mind.

Your attitude toward money is erratic; not understanding where it comes from, you're either profligate or stingy, depending not upon the figures in your bank account but upon your mood. If you're feeling optimistic, you'll spend wildly, euphorically convinced that more will turn up somehow, from somewhere; when worried or depressed, you'll cling to every penny, just as irrationally convinced that starvation is right around the corner.

You're prey to all kinds of baseless fears: an unreasoning dread of contagion and infection, of suddenly losing all your money in a crash, of being abandoned by all your friends and lovers at once, of becoming a vegetable overnight from some incurable crippling disease. Still more pervasive is the fear of falling under the influence of some evil will, its inevitable and helpless victim.

And your weak sense of cause and effect often does put you at the mercy of a whole shady underworld of fortune tellers, clairvoyants, and psychic healers. Any flashy necromancer will find his most gullible, porous-minded subjects among the endo ectos who sit open-mouthed at his feet. He doesn't even have to be flashy, just frightening. Nancy, for instance, a Radcliffe *summa cum laude*, a poet and critic, was unlucky enough to cross the path of a filthy, toothless gypsy soothsayer with not more but pathetically fewer powers, magical or otherwise, than almost anyone, who nonetheless was able to persuade Nancy that unless she turned over most of her income to the gypsy, her mother back in Iowa would die a horrible lingering death. To meet this hag's extortions Nancy beggared herself for months; she'd be doing it still if one day the hag hadn't disappeared.

But while you may fall easy victim to charlatans, you do have a genuine feeling for the uncanny. Often you're in closer touch with the spirit world than with waking reality. Many of you have psychic powers, or believe you do; at any rate, you feel surrounded by ghosts or by spectral emanations from the living. To you, it's the absent ones who are most vibrantly present: your lover's wife, your mistress's husband, the dead child, the vanished father. You're sensitive to hauntings; past and future are both more vivid to you than the present. You prefer living in your imagination anyway, with a past that's a manageable memory, a future that's a dream.

You have a special sensitivity to houses; to you, every old

house gives off unmistakable vibrations of welcome or enmity. In certain moods you become convinced that you're simultaneously in touch with everything that ever lived in or around the house, all the generations of people and animals, even plants; the specter of an ancient elm that was blasted by lightning a hundred years ago will speak to you in a dream. You're often mildly ill with headaches or colds, and enjoy the feeling while you're lying in bed that the spirit of the house is watching protectively over you.

Living as you do in a permanent state of passive receptivity, you're susceptible to invasion from the spirit world; you make ideal mediums, conduits for the psychic energies of others. Objects, too, have a malign life of their own, sometimes seeming almost to rise up and attack you: The furniture appears to breathe; a flower becomes a devouring mouth—the whole external world of things is full of menace. Certain other objects become invested with talismanic powers; endo ectos are great collectors of charms and amulets, lucky coins, Egyptian turquoises.

You take the universe personally; it's one of the many ways in which you remain childlike all your life. To you there's no such thing as an objective event resulting from the operation of some natural law; everything that happens, happens *to you* and carries a personal message. Life is full of signs and portents: a flight of birds in a certain pattern, a sequence of license plate numbers, the shape of a cloud, a sign in a shop window, a swirl of fallen leaves. The Ouija board speaks to you, too, and your passed-on Uncle Henry never fails to come through with a greeting and a stock market tip.

Your dread of falling under some baleful influence that will take over your life is part of a general suspicion of being surrounded by powers, visible and invisible, benevolent and evil, that you can't control—beginning with the force of gravity. But you're also eager in a way to surrender to such influences, and you'll always take a hint from some seedy stranger sooner than advice from your family doctor or stockbroker. You have an odd attraction to the sordid and squalid; the shabbier the room in which your fortune is told, the grimier the hand whose palm you cross with silver, the greasier the cards, the more imbecilic the mutterings, the more absolute your faith.

Flamboyant Anarchy

Even the most fastidious among you will harbor an affinity for slightly sinister low life, for nightclubs and bars that cater to "special tastes," for the dubious and *louche*. For you feel that your own existence is more than a little absurd; not for you, people and events that are bright, direct, forthright. You're drawn to the shadowy and suspect, as expressing your own self-deprecation. You have a penchant for perversions, especially masochism—a fearful fascination with pain. With such slender physiological defenses, your terror of pain is well justified, but nevertheless you often seek it out— apparently on the theory that initiating the experience will give you some control over it. How wrong you are about that, you learn very fast; it's always your flesh that feels the bite of the iron, the burn of the whip.

Your sense of humor is whimsical, particularly delighted by the ridiculous side of human pretensions. You, who have so little control over anything, early acquire a sharp eye for those lapses in people who are excessively confident of their control: the smear of lipstick on the face that believes itself perfect, the dribble on the chin of the pompous chairman, all those involuntary little grimaces, grunts, and gurgles that give us away.

Your spirit is often teasing, mocking, subversive. Some of the most talented—or perhaps merely desperate—among you find a defiant solution to your low endowment of meso, depriving it of its force by making an exaggerated display of everything that meso is not, and that it despises: wit, fantasy, playfulness; substituting verbal audacity for physical recklessness, grace for power, form for content.

The trick is to undercut meso solidity and strength by making them seem witless and ponderous, catching them off balance by deploying dexterity against superior force, as in a judo flip. Your style is light, glancing. You wield a rapier; the meso, a club. Where he lumbers, you dance, converting your physical insecurity into a balancing act, always testing the limits of outrageousness, hoping with each caper to go too "far out."

It's a triumph of style over substance, manner over matter, and it often goes along with a refusal to recognize meso patriarchal authority, to become a mature, "responsible" adult—to grow up at all. You rebellious endo ectos defiantly choose to remain perpetual Peter Pans, disporting forever in a sunlit, anarchic adolescence.

Skimming over the surface with a view from higher up than those who walk upon it, or crawl, you see more, or at least you see differently. You're rarely enlisted into the ranks of reliable functionaries, the carriers-out of routine; your contributions are more likely to be surprising stabs of perception, the revelation to another of his own heart in a sudden piercing shaft of understanding: "The truth is, you don't want to take that scholarship now that you've won it, do you?" "You're not in love with Ronald; why are you marrying him?" "They're trying to push you into living with your father and step-mother, but you're still mourning your own mother, aren't you?"

Beauty Is Truth

Your sensitivity is usually matched by an equal sympathy, especially for suffering. But you respond so emotionally to any crisis, you sometimes seem to be taking the tragedy of others away from them, playing the game of "more sensitive than thou." "When Philip got the diagnosis of cancer, the one person I was sure I could lean on was Andy, always so warm, so concerned. But no. He couldn't even come and visit us without bursting into tears, let alone help me out later at the hospital. He felt so sorry for *himself*, having a friend to whom such an awful thing had happened! And the treatment was worse than the disease, he kept saying unhelpfully. He couldn't stand the sight of Philip after his hair fell out. Finally I just told him to stay away; it upset Philip too much to see *him* so upset."

You're the most refined and subtle of connoisseurs, collectors of sensation, with an exquisite receptiveness to every form of beauty: flowers, music, perfumes, poetry, painting. Few of you can resist the attraction of the ballet, which combines so many of these experiences in the most highly stylized form, and which offers to the physically inept and unstable the spectacle of bodies disciplined to the most perfect and expressive control.

And while many of you are religious, you're attracted to the spiritual life more for its music, for the quality of the art it inspires, rather than the meaning behind its ritual. You're likely to become a convert to one of the religions of the East, or to Catholicism; in fact, to you the Catholic Mass is almost a kind of ballet.

You can be highly successful as museum curators, editors, critics, decorators, book and antique dealers, designers of fabric or jewelry—careers that make use of your superior taste, your discriminating eye. Your capacity for receiving impressions is very great, your ability to act upon them slight. You're aesthetes who respond intensely to art, but don't as a rule create it—with some notable exceptions, such as Marcel Proust.

When you do become artists, however, you seldom attempt to produce any sustained or structurally imposing work, or arrive at some ultimate "meaning." You tend not to see life steadily and whole; you're mosaicists, dealing in intermittent flickers and sparks. You're light but penetrating, sharp, accurate. It's only in the realm of the imagination that you can rule, and inadequate as you may be to the demands of real life, in the constructs of the mind you can be hard and exact. You blow bubbles, but those iridescent globes sometimes float amazingly far, and outlast timber and stone.

It is very characteristic of you, though, to be dissatisfied with your talents, however rare and valuable. You suspect that the rest of the world considers you a lightweight, and you resent it. Your gift is precisely *not* to weigh heavily, and usually you're sensible enough to recognize this. But sometimes you succumb to envy of those who create more imposing structures, whether of art or love, and such envy can become corrosive.

A Taste of Ashes

Rosemary met Gordon when as a young actress she landed a small part in one of his plays. She attracted some favorable attention, but was never serious about a career in the theater; her dread of its competitive stresses far outweighed any pleasure she felt as a performer. Her appeal, as an actress and a woman, lay in a dreamy remoteness, a veiled, tremulous quality that led one critic to compare her to a startled fawn; another, to a water nymph. It lent her a misty charm in private life, but was a little too delicate to project on the stage, and somehow eluded the camera as well.

So she decided to let Gordon, who had been strenuously pursuing her from East Coast to West and back, win his prize and marry her, and take care of her ever after.

It seemed that he would be able to do this in style, for he was writing one hit after another, had won two Tonys in a row. An essential factor in his success was his unique production team, which consisted of Jerry, his producer, and Doug, who directed most of his plays. These three had been buddies since high school, when they'd vowed to crash the big time together. They had a strong, close, working camaraderie that had survived early poverty, bad mistakes, and a succession of failures.

Now those hard years had begun to pay off at last. Important stars were eager to read for them. The most recent script to go into production looked as if it was going to be the biggest hit yet. Gordon came home every evening excited and exultant.

Curious, Rosemary dropped in on a rehearsal one day, sitting unnoticed in the back. Everyone was moving purposefully about, wholly absorbed in what they were doing. She felt out of it—not only of the play, but of her own life. Watching Doug block out a scene with Jo Featherstone, the two of them as intent as a pair of dancers, Rosemary remembered a line from a part she had once played in summer stock—"The truth is, Sonia, I was everywhere just a passing face"—and a tear fell on her new Saint Laurent beige silk skirt.

Gordon, Jerry, and Doug scarcely needed to speak to know what the others were thinking, but nobody cared what she thought, or whether she thought anything at all. The center of Gordon's life wasn't with her; it was there in the theater, with them. Gradually Rosemary began spending most of her days at the theater, too, and before long she was planting insidious little seeds of doubt. Was she merely testing the strength of Gordon's bond with the other two, or intentionally undermining it?

Whatever her motives, every now and then she would insert a slim, sharp fingernail into an invisible crevice, each time widening and deepening the crack. "Of course he must know what he's doing—but speaking just as an observer, darling, I wonder why Doug lets Featherstone chop off the ends of your lines like that. . . . Whatever possessed Jerry to hire Thea to do costumes? You can certainly tell she's never done anything but musicals before; all those red bugle beads are *blinding*. . . . I hope you don't mind my mentioning these things; I just want them to do right by your wonderful play." Next it was: "I just can't bear to see them ruin your wonderful play." Then: "I think Doug is a tiny bit jealous of you, and who can blame him? You're the one with the creative genius; he's just an interpreter. A parasite, really. . . . It's amazing the way Jerry's making a bundle off your talent, and what is he contributing but bad judgment?"

Why did she do it? What demon of self-destruction made her erode her own security? For Gordon *was* her security, all she had. She never knew why, because she never admitted to herself what she was doing. Afterward, all three were to say that it was probably time anyway for them to go their separate ways; that no partnership lasted forever; that after the final blowup each realized how deeply dissatisfied he'd been all along.

Still, the fact remained that before Rosemary entered the scene, there had been something firm, even if it was only a facade, and when she finished there was nothing left but ashes. Even her own marriage was consumed, along with everything else.

Well-being for Endo Ectos

Roots in Reality

Your sense of being about to be overwhelmed by alien and hostile forces stems not from any such reality "out there," but from a feeling of powerlessness within. But if you insist on handing your life over to others to run for you, you're having it only on their terms. Yet to you, almost any task—especially any that involves independent action, let alone taking responsibility for others—looms terrifyingly.

Your two greatest traps: procrastination and dependence. As control slips further and further out of your hands, your life becomes increasingly disordered and chaotic and you become more and more fearful as you lose what little initiative you had in taking care of yourself. Often there's a remarkable contrast between your efficiency at work—because there you can rely upon a structure impersonally imposed upon you from outside yourself—and the mess your private life is in.

And it can only get worse; there's no self-limiting feedback system built into this process. The deeper you sink, the more difficult it is to climb back; your means of saving yourself have themselves been undermined. So you blur your vision, self-protectively, and the more desperate your state, the dreamier you become.

What you need is to develop inner self-confidence; to strengthen your will, in the old-fashioned phrase; to take charge of your life; to become less dependent and more self-sufficient. If you've never called upon your inner resources, why should you believe you've got any? The prospect of relying upon yourself alone for anything probably fills you with panic. In developing inner strength, it's important to *start small*. You don't have to solve all your problems at once. *Any* move in the direction of self-sufficiency and independence will increase your capacity to make others. The important thing is to make a beginning, to start reversing that nightmare slide into helplessness.

- The key to getting control over your life is simple: DO IT NOW. Whatever it is. Simply to stop procrastinating reduces immediately the jittery feeling that comes from a mind that's always running ahead of its body, so that dread infects every prospect. If you've got a meal to cook, a paper to write, any task to start or finish, *do it now.* Instead of yielding to the temptation to put it off until you're churning with nervous anxiety and relying on *that* to propel you, break it down into its components and deal with each of them one at a time. Every job, every project seems overwhelming if you look at the whole thing at once: "I've got to write a fifty-page report by next Thursday!" And your panic may be so paralyzing that Thursday will arrive without your having even made a start. Analyzing each task into its elements shows you that each one of them is doable by itself; do them one by one, and you've got the whole.

- The feeling that chaos is about to overcome you stems in large part from the erratic quality of your energy and your wildly irregular habits—if you can be said to have any habits at all. Order saves energy, even creates it by establishing calm, harmony, security. A regular schedule for meals, relaxation, exercise, and sleep imparts a rhythm to your days that in itself gives you a structure to lean on.

- Depression and fatigue go hand in hand with you; a nap, a break, a day off always lifts your spirits, is your best restorative.

- Learn to say no, clearly and definitely. And don't look longingly back. There's always something to be said for the choice you didn't make—but once you've made it, it's over. Move on!

- Your imagination is overdeveloped at the expense of the practical side. Taking a course in money management, helping a local politician run for election, learning how to make simple electrical repairs, even learning how to drive a car helps put down roots in reality, can transform the way you see yourself. And acquiring competence in practical skills is a great alleviator of anxiety.

Food: Sweetness and Light

Even if you succumb to lethargy, you may get soft, but you don't accumulate much excess weight. You do however have one weakness: a raging sweet tooth. You're too often tempted to bypass nourishing food and go for the dessert. What you probably crave is not the sugar itself, but the energy rush you get from the sudden jump in your blood sugar—which can be dangerous. When you eat sweets on an empty stomach, blood sugar levels rise steeply and fast, plummet soon after just as fast, sometimes even causing you to black out.

- You can satisfy your sweet tooth with the sugar in fruit, which delivers energy more steadily and safely, and is just as delicious as a gooey dessert. Try the lovely Italian *frulatto di frutto*, a fruit shake you can make in seconds in a blender:

  In the blender container put 1 cup whole or skim milk, 1 tablespoon honey, then about 1½ cups of any combination of the following, pitted or cored and cut up in medium-size pieces, with the skin on all but the last three: purple or red plums, apples, bing cherries, green grapes, raspberries, strawberries, blueberries, peaches, nectarines, apricots, bananas, mango, papaya. Blend for a minute at high speed.

- You hate the heavy sensation of fat in the stomach, prefer lighter, low-fat foods. But your protein needs, as with all ectos, tend to be high, and most animal protein is also high in fat. Look to vegetable sources for most of your protein. An excellent one is tofu, or bean curd, a protean food that can assume almost any flavor and texture; in Chinese dishes it adds creaminess, in salads gives subtlety to the crunchy greens; sauteed, it's like crisp French fries. It can assume any flavor, from shrimp to strawberry, goes hot or sour, and tofu ice cream gives you sweetness with one of the highest protein values per ounce of any food.

- Be sure to get plenty of fluids. You dehydrate easily, but your small stomach will quickly feel bloated if you drink too much at once. Sipping often throughout the day is the best way to satisfy your need for fluids. Drink vegetable and fruit juices (with no sugar added) rather than coffee or colas.

Exercise: Easy Does It

Building a sturdier, more dependable body not only improves your physical stamina, it's like creating a new and stronger self. The will is, after all, a matter of muscles; if you can't even support yourself upright very well, how can you act with confidence out in the world?

- If you're completely out of condition, the first thing is to get yourself moving in some sort of systematic way on some sort of schedule—what form the movement takes doesn't much matter. The easiest is usually walking. If you have access to a swimming pool, alternate walking with swimming three or four times a week. If you're very weak, try exercising in intervals, as follows:

  Take as your goal to spend, for instance, fifteen minutes on foot or in the water, and start out as briskly as you feel comfortable. When you tire, slow down to a stroll, or float in the water, until you can resume again at the faster pace. Keep alternating faster- with slower-paced movement until you've done your quarter of an hour. Gradually the faster-paced periods will become longer, the resting periods shorter. But try to keep in motion to some degree for the entire time. (Of course if you feel dizzy or seriously out of breath, take a rest.)
  As you become stronger, the total period will lengthen too. Your eventual goal should be at least half an hour three or four times a week—but take your time getting there. Do not push yourself to a point of fatigue that makes you miss the next exercise period.
  Stay within a zone of reasonable comfort—but *keep moving*.

- Your abdominal and lower back muscles are weak and need systematic strengthening exercises (see the ones described on page 89). In addition, you need to strengthen your upper back; you tend to be round-shouldered and to slump, which not only is painful to the upper back but adds to the pressure on your lower spine. Here's an exercise that is difficult to do, but is a wonderful upper-back strengthener that also benefits the whole back, buttocks, and even thighs:

Lie on your stomach with your heels hooked under a heavy piece of furniture (or have someone hold them down). Your forehead is touching the floor. Place your hands on the back of your neck so the fingertips touch, elbows straight out to the sides. Contracting your upper back, lift your chest as far off the floor as you can. (If you can't lift it at all, don't worry; it's the effort that counts. Keep trying.) Return to the floor; repeat. Do as many as you can, increasing gradually from five to fifty.

- Strength, flexibility, and endurance are the three requirements for muscular fitness; you're fairly flexible but low in strength and endurance. Aerobics (walking or swimming) builds endurance. To develop strength, alternate your aerobic workouts with a calisthenics class two or three times a week. Here again, the point is not to try to keep up with the others, but just to keep going; do the exercises as best you can, and don't get discouraged. Persistence is far more important than form; improvement will come quickly if you keep trying.

- As the exercises get easier, gradually add light wrist and ankle weights (½ pound at a time) to increase resistance, build strength faster.

- A good aerobics dance class is one of the best workouts around, and can be a lot of fun even if you're out of condition, provided you don't worry about doing the routine perfectly. Just keep moving to the music. Remember, the instructor is already in terrific shape; you're only starting to get there.

9. MESO ECTOS:
Lithe and Wiry

Who You Are

In you quirky individualists, ecto is dominant, with meso secondary and endo the lowest of the three. Wherever endo is low, there's also a lack of comfort, of conformity, of compromise. You're restless people, perpetually dissatisfied seekers, continually scanning the horizon for some answer or fulfillment that lies beyond.

Quick, sharp, fine, you're like cut crystal, with a pure, high ring. Often you'll exhibit a reckless bravery that pushes you way out beyond your depth—and your strength; the temptation to flirt with death can sometimes become irresistible. Not that you're fearless; on the contrary, you're often terrified, even of ordinary daily life—perhaps especially of that. But most of all, you're afraid of failing to rise to a challenge.

You're most sharply challenged by cruelty or injustice. Even as a child, whenever you see an unequal fight—a bully beating up a smaller kid, a gang against a lone person or animal—you'll rush into the fray, arms and legs windmilling furiously, emerging at the end bruised and tattered but shining-eyed: You've struck a blow. "It's not fair!" is your constant cry; later, "It's not *right*!" All your life you go leaping to the defense of the underdog, the victim. In disproportionate numbers you're to be found in the ragged Republican cadres of Spain, on the buses in the back roads of Mississippi, in the field hospitals of Central America.

It's not the specific cause that arouses you so much as the threat to freedom. You're never slaves to an ideology; whenever the revolutionary vision hardens into a new conformity, you'll rebel in turn against that. You're the lovers of opposition, of the minority view, the enemies of every status quo. Nor is it political injustice alone that excites your passions; the petty constraints of living, the claims of family, friends, career, can seem just as oppressive, intolerable limitations on your liberty.

In you, the strongest impulse is to move. Happiness means to be, figuratively if not in fact, on the road. One situation after another you experience as a prison, feeling yourself trapped and suffocating in a job, at a party, in a marriage, a car, a supermarket checkout line. Whenever your freedom of movement is blocked, you can plunge into panic or a rage; your worst nightmare is to feel bound, pinioned. *Escape* is what you long for; not love, or a safe harbor; not arrival, but departure. Or rather, not the departure itself but the freedom at any time to move on.

Those who have managed to get close to you know better than to clutch or cling; you'll only struggle until you pull free and make your getaway. It's no good making an appeal to your pity, either; that only arouses your contempt. One must be willing to let you go, even conspire in your going; then you may hang around for a while—but you make no promises.

You're inveterate travelers. It's as if every change of scene lends you a new identity, as if by continuous motion through space you can manage to keep evolving, in perpetual self-renewal. To those who protest that at some point in life you've got to "put down some roots," you'll retort, "A person is not a tree."

Rebirth in the Desert

You're not people who cherish the known quantity, well loved for its cozy familiarity. Hankering impatiently after novelty and change, never content with any form that is fixed or final, you refuse to settle for anything less than continual rebirth and metamorphosis. You resent all attempts to pin you down, to define you. "I can't imagine you ever becoming a forest ranger" or "a medical missionary; you're such a typical hausfrau" or "intellectual"—say something like that to you once, and there will never be a chance to say it again. Even defining adjectives annoy you: "I'm *not* high-strung. Sure, I get annoyed sometimes, but that doesn't mean I'm *that kind of person!*" "How *dare* you call me a perfectionist? Just because I like to do things *right!*"

You can be deeply, self-protectively secretive; at best, your emotional flow is never smooth, always erratic and unpredictable. One moment you'll retreat into a brooding inwardness, going deep inside yourself and pulling down the shades; the next, you'll suddenly flare out, a fierce flame, alarming in its suddenness and vehemence.

Despite your headlong impatience, you age slowly, stay young until late in life. And all your life there's something unfinished about you, something latent. You seem never quite to reach fruition; you've always got more changes up your sleeve. A common life pattern is a long, slow early development, then adult achievement, and then retreat. Much later, often when least expected, you emerge from the desert, or retirement, and lead the company or the country once again, sometimes in a completely new direction. You have a phoenixlike ability to return over and over again from defeat or exile. Your cycles of renewal seem infinite; just when you've been confidently written off for good, that's the moment when you make your most triumphant comeback.

This is true for meso ecto public figures at every point along the spectrum. There's Marlene Dietrich, stigmatized as "box-office poison" in 1942, who thereupon took herself overseas to entertain the GIs, launching a whole new career—and who did it yet again in late middle age in the 1960s, this time as a solo nightclub performer. And there's Charles de Gaulle, the unknown army officer who arose out of nowhere in 1940 to become the solitary symbol of Free France, who led her into peace, was rejected, defeated, retired, spent twelve years "in the wilderness," then rose once again to lead the country through the Algerian crisis.

You're impelled by inner imperatives that often seem to have little to do with external circumstances, and in fact your entire relationship with the outer world is usually very tentative and uneasy. You can attach yourself to certain things or people with a frightening intensity that seems to have nothing to do with any quality in them—and in fact it hasn't. It's projected from within you, expressing some wholly private cluster of associations.

Someone who finds himself the object of your desire or dislike will feel as though an irrational and irresistible power has grabbed him by the hair. "What have I done to deserve this?" he cries, in terror or delight, or both. The answer, of course, is nothing. You have a way of loading the present with emotional baggage from the past, which makes your behavior a mystery to those who don't know the source of its energy. Anyone who happens to attract your attention when your charge of feeling is approaching the flash point may feel as though he's wandered into the path of a tornado.

"Vivian. Ah, yes, Vivian," sighs Steve. "A girl who was mined. My arrival in Vivian's life detonated it all. Everything that had happened to her—her father's desertion, her uncle's seduction of her a couple of years after that, the sadism of the brute she married—I was all the men in her life who had done her in. And that was just about all the men she'd ever had anything to do with.

"In the middle of the night she'd wake up and cling to me as though she were drowning, imploring me never to leave her. But next day when she came home from work, she'd be spoiling for a fight. She had no idea who I was—just another oppressor. The only way to cope with her rages was to lie low and let them blow themselves out, but she wouldn't permit that. She'd corner me in the bedroom or the kitchen and force a confrontation.

"Soon it got to the point where she'd attack me physically. She used to wear what I called combat jewelry—sharp-edged rings, bracelets with spikes—and she'd pummel me with her fists. One night she pulled off a heavy chain belt she was wearing that had a sort of egg-shaped amethyst pendant and started swinging it around her head like a bola, screaming, 'I'll kill you all, you sons of bitches!'

"I knew she didn't mean it personally, but it was my personal skull that was about to get cracked. It was at that point I decided our romance had cooled. I managed to duck the rock long enough to get out of the house, and soon after that I moved out altogether. I had always told myself that at least life with Viv was never boring, but I didn't need that much excitement."

The Edge of the Abyss

It's difficult for others, especially endos, to understand the complexity of your relationship with the world. Endos can lean upon the comforting solidity and *thereness* of external reality, can draw strength from it, in a way that meso ectos cannot. You live much further inside yourself, and you're elated or downcast, optimistic or despairing, according to the shifts in the tides of your inner world. Sudden and strong reversal in these tides is a characteristic pattern; you tend to be manic-depressives. And when you're depressed, everything becomes gray, flat, empty. As meso ecto Sylvia Plath wrote, "The horror is the sudden folding up and away of the phenomenal world, leaving nothing. Just rags. Human rooks which say: Fraud."

This dreaded state is sometimes the precursor of a suicide attempt. You have a tremendous capacity for self-regeneration and can always, as long as you want to, pull yourself back from the abyss. But you seem to spend a lot of time clinging to the edge and peering fascinatedly over it.

And if the real world ceases to correspond to your concept of what it ought to be, you will retreat into your imagination, a realm no less actual than the world out there. You won't settle for an imperfect reality; a meso ecto woman who can't find a man to match her dreams will often not marry at all, preferring to live in a fantasy of an ideal love. No endo woman could understand this; she'd rather have a flesh-and-blood man who may be a little rough with her and is even unfaithful now and then, but who also gives her a nice cuddle when she needs it, and earns a decent living. Endos always prefer something they can "hold on to"; what you hold on to is your dreams. Compared with the power of fantasy, the outer world seems insubstantial.

Naked Lasers

You're dedicated loners. Whatever your situation—married ten years with a gaggle of kids; embedded, as a public figure, in a matrix of secretaries, press people, aides-de-camp; or locked into togetherness at an office from morning till night— you nevertheless always stand a little apart. You're the opposite of gregarious, uneasy in any group just because it *is* a group. You tend to view yourself and everyone around you with ironic detachment. "Stay out of my space," you always seem to be saying, and others instinctively do. Very early you acquire a quick, cutting tongue; even your parents soon learn to respect its edge. People tend to be circumspect in their approach to you, and let you make the advances. Secretive, jealous, and proud, you're slightly derisive, mocking observers of your own doings, too, finding them more than a little ridiculous.

You most often prefer to work alone. You're unhappy as collaborators or partners, still more so as subordinates— unless you're part of an organization that lets you operate with a minimum of daily interference, like Sam Goldwyn, who remarked, "Even when I had partners, I was always an independent."

Your energies have a different rhythm from that of endos or mesos. You're very fast, very impatient; you can't bear any hindrance. You thrive on short bouts of intense concentration, driving yourself to the limit with lashings of nervous energy, then collapsing flat-out—a cycle that seems to repeat itself indefinitely. In your work habits, as in everything else, you have your own way of doing things.

You're best at carrying out an assignment that leaves you a free hand to work out the details of its execution. "Find out what the hell's going on down at the River Neige plant. They're screwing up, and I can't figure out why or who's responsible. You'll have to go down there and take a look around—but don't let them know you came from the home office. You decide what story to give them—but if they find out you're spying on them, it'll be your head that rolls." And you do make excellent spies, clandestine information gatherers; as alert observers and permanent outsiders, you see plenty that others miss.

"I don't care how you do it, but I've got to have those reports in hand at nine o'clock Monday morning. Recruit anybody and anything you need; just get them done." You love this kind of assignment, which lets you bring a burning-glass concentration to bear on a single objective—which for that moment becomes the only thing in the world, whether it's a romance, a chess problem, an argument, a lost dog, or buying a pair of boots.

In your surroundings you prefer naked simplicity, clean, pure. You like bare, white surfaces, austere angles. Ideally you'd have a house on a height, perched on a rock overlooking the sea, all glass—a house with a view in every direction, as near as possible to living out of doors, an eagle's nest. Not for you a little cabin nestled in the forest, or any sense of enclosure at all. If you must have walls, you prefer them bare, like the rest of the house—except perhaps for a few souvenirs of your travels. But every object should stimulate an image or a thought; you're impatient with anything of merely "sentimental" value which only clutters up your space.

Hidden Wounds

Your leading faculty is vision—a dissecting, analytical vision. You're drawn to careers as naturalists, pathologists, photographers, exploring each subject that comes into view with a detached but probing curiosity. You like to make a solitary descent into the heart of the thing—as though diving deeply enough into it will force it to render up its essence to your inquisitive lens.

You're extremely secretive, always holding some important part of yourself in reserve. Often what you're concealing is pain. You have an immense capacity for suffering—so great sometimes that it becomes almost a source of shame, a guilty secret. It's not that you're masochistic so much as that experience cuts deep, and lastingly.

In your intimacy with pain you can give an impression of having "been there," known the worst, faced the worst, to an extent that is independent of experience. While your life may seem from the outside to have been a sustained soar to the top, you nonetheless possess an unusual instinct for suffering—the suffering of others no less than your own. You may flinch from painful memories, agonize over the future, but you don't run away from the threat of pain. You have a gritty steadfastness, a stoicism you can call upon when you're up against it. You'll never evade any problem as long as it has a possible solution; you'll face up to every crisis if there's something to be done, or borne. But if you perceive that defeat or humiliation is built into the situation from the outset, you'll walk straight away from it, with nothing but contempt for those who stay.

When you feel betrayed, or struck in your pride, you respond with icy withdrawal. But in any less extreme confrontation you're highly combative, verbally at least, furiously argumentative, especially over just those subjects that cannot be resolved through argument: religion, politics, ethics, taste.

You think of yourself as superior to social convention, scornful of "good manners," despising as hypocritical the soothing rituals of etiquette. You're given to speaking uncomfortable truths just as they occur to you, unconcerned about anyone's feelings. At the same time, though, you also fancy yourself as a wily, Machiavellian schemer and intriguer, shrewdly and coldbloodedly calculating your advantage over an opponent. You think you're subtle and devious, and while it's true that you know well enough where the power lies, how to flatter, what to conceal, how to time your strokes, when it comes to exploiting these skills for your own ends, you trip over yourself. It's not that you lack cunning, but that you betray yourself in an untimely spasm of integrity.

You'll go to endless trouble to plan your strategy and then, when you've at last managed to maneuver the president of the company you'd like to work for into sitting next to you at the dinner party, you'll choose that moment to burst into an attack on his product, his judgment, his morals. "What on earth got into you? After all you went through to get him into position to make your pitch?"

"I don't know, I just wanted to wipe that smug look off his fat pig face. So okay, I lost my head."

It's you who will charge a police line with your bare fists; who, at the end of the job interview, will abruptly let the personnel manager in on some frank truths about his interviewing technique; who, on the verge of getting your first commission from the most important picture magazine, will blurt out to the editor your opinion of his editorial policy and his taste in photographs. You'll overthrow every one of your own most carefully laid plans in one slashing moment of truth.

An ornery meso ecto possesses an uncommon talent for bringing together the most bitterly divided factions in any community, uniting them in hatred of him. At your worst, you exhibit a puritanical self-righteousness that infuriates everyone, on every side. "I never thought the day would come when I'd agree with Charlie Evans on anything, but the morning after that faculty meeting when Warren got up and denounced each one of us individually as a corrupt sell-out to the trustees, then tore up the proposal we'd labored over and walked out, Charlie and I met for coffee and talked over the Warren problem like old buddies."

Traveling Light

You're always ready to walk out, not only when it seems to you that principles are being betrayed, but sometimes merely out of restlessness. You form passionate attachments which you shed as soon as you feel the urge to transcend that particular state of being, like sloughing off a dead skin. And you're as ruthless in cutting loose when you're finished as you were attached before. You're jealous and possessive of everything that touches you closely, but the moment it no longer does, you turn completely cold. It's as though you're on a lifelong search for some ineffable something that you locate first in this one, then in that, ridding yourself of the old without a backward thought as you pursue your quest.

At one point in her life Kate hurls herself into a stony-eyed battle for possession of the Royal Doulton dinner service that had been willed to her mother but stored with Aunt Clara, and which Aunt Clara's daughters now refuse to surrender. Kate fights for these pieces of china as though they were saints' relics, and after a long and bloody fight finally wins them. But a couple of years later, when she moves to another city, she forgets to take them with her, leaves them all behind on the top shelf of a kitchen closet.

Similarly, you never seem really to inhabit your clothes. Every once in a while the urge seizes you to be well-dressed for a change, and you embark on an orgy of shopping that your perfectionist zeal turns into a hell-bent mission for the ideal hat, the dream dress, the perfectly tailored suit. But the only time it fits is the first few minutes; immediately it begins mysteriously to wrinkle and sag, hanging away from your body as though it knew how fundamentally indifferent you were to it.

You never become immersed in your own existence, never fully identify yourself with the social and professional roles you enact. One always has the sense that these roles are like your clothes, at best transitory disguises, ill-fitting costumes and masks that may be thrown off at any moment. "She's a young mother getting a law degree"; "he's an electrical engineer"; but one has the uneasy feeling that sooner or later you'll tire of these identities, and that when you do you'll leave them behind just as carelessly as you do everything else. You're bolters, not stickers; when the time comes, families, lovers, entire lives to which you've seemed utterly committed suddenly become mere interference, impediments cluttering and blocking the road to your true goal.

And just what that goal is—well, that's never quite so clear as your impatient certainty that the objects and connections of dailiness are getting in the way of reaching it. The goal sometimes seems to be nothing more than simply to cast off all the paraphernalia of ordinary human life, like ballast from a balloon, and rise to some transcendent state of total purity and freedom.

It's a meso ecto who, hitherto an impeccable housewife and mother, suddenly runs off with a country-and-western singer from a touring band, to the stupefaction of all. "Emptied out our checking account and took off in the clothes she stood up in," says Patricia's husband Bill, still stunned. And that wasn't the end of it, either. They heard indirectly that after a few weeks she ditched the singer too. Left him in the middle of the night in a motel in Little Rock. Light as the two of them were traveling, it wasn't light enough for Patricia. She seems to have hitched her way from there to the West Coast; at least, she told the vending machine repairman who picked her up somewhere in Nevada that she was on her way to Calcutta to join Mother Teresa.

"And do you think she so much as lifted a finger when the other families in our congregation were taking in Salvadoran refugees? Why, she never even *went* to church! If Mother Teresa makes the mistake of counting on Pat for anything— well, I just feel sorry for Mother Teresa, that's all."

"No," says a friend, "we haven't heard the last of Patricia. Somebody will have seen her wandering off barefoot into the desert, carrying a burning cross. And to think that she was senior class secretary at Akron High."

Dive to the Heights

At least once in your life you'll find yourself at the brink, having lost everything, or having at last succeeded in getting rid of it all. At that point, in one final surge of energy, you'll gamble your life—and having taken the ultimate risk, rise up again triumphant. The plunge to the bottom shoots you back up to the heights; it's as though you've found an answer down there, in the depths of the ocean, on the other side of the looking glass—but you have to risk death to find it. Only in extreme crisis, it seems, do you find your truth, and anything less absolute is that much less true.

"*Perdre,*" said the poet Apollinaire, "*mais perdre vraiment, pour laisser place à la trouvaille.*" Lose—but lose for good, to make room for the find.

A meso ecto statesman whose career illustrates many traits

of the type was Charles de Gaulle. A solitary figure even at the height of power, he was animated all his life by one single idea, an unwavering flame: the glory of France. "All my life I have thought of France in a certain way," his memoirs begin, ". . . like the princess in the fairy stories or the Madonna in the frescoes, as dedicated to an exalted and exceptional destiny."

The extraordinary events of 1940—when this unknown soldier, defying orders from his superior officers to surrender to the Germans, escaped alone across the Channel to England, carrying with him nothing but the vision of a free and undefeated France—became the legend out of which after the war France revived her nearly extinct national pride. But at the time de Gaulle had no firm support from anyone, not even Churchill, whose backing was crucial but who frequently wavered, and who never, throughout de Gaulle's struggle to establish his legitimacy as the spokesman for Free France, ceased to look for someone else, *anyone* else, to represent the French government in exile.

De Gaulle hung on and triumphed in the end because, although haughty, cold, and repellent to many, remote and obsessed with notions of "grandeur," he stubbornly clung to the impossible idea that one obscure and unpopular, but uncompromising, man could embody the spirit of the nation and rally her demoralized forces.

Several times he was close to suicide: once in Bordeaux, just before his desperate flight to England ("I seemed to myself, alone as I was and deprived of everything, like a man on the shore of an ocean, proposing to swim across"), and once in Dakar, when it appeared that Churchill would finally yield to strong political pressure to abandon him. Yet de Gaulle's faith in his unique destiny pulled him through every crisis. Throughout his career he was true to the conviction he held in 1940, that "limited and alone though I was, and precisely because I was so, I had to climb to the heights and never then to come down."

Well-being for Meso Ectos

Breathing Space

Most of your difficulties, especially with others, arise from your too narrow focus of feeling. Your emotions tend to be sharp, hot; intensity is your natural state, but you exclude too much. The laserlike concentration you bring to bear on the ordinary issues of life is appropriate only to microsurgery.

You overreact to everything; all your responses are too quick. You rush, especially, to accuse, with the result that people soon cease to have faith in your judgment, feeling that it's too harsh, too rigid, and often too self-righteous. You want passionately to be taken seriously, but the best way to achieve that is to broaden the scope of your sympathies, so others can trust that you're not merely out to annihilate the opposition.

Your body is always under excessive tension, which you experience as anxiety—and which in turn makes you unwilling to release the tension. You're afraid to let go—but it's the tension itself that causes the fear. The way to deal with these tensions, which are largely unconscious, is to bring them into awareness; then it is possible to release them.

Awareness is your forte; you can't have too much of it, and you'll be fascinated to learn how much of yourself is blocked to your own consciousness through a relentless, numbing muscular grip that has cut your range of feeling and response down to a tiny fraction of what's possible. For you're the most sensitive, the most finely calibrated of any body type, capable of the subtlest, most delicate discriminations of feeling and sensation. But all of it is blunted by the tensions that make you bear down too hard on yourself and everyone else. Emotionally you tend to swing between extremes of irritability and numbness.

• What you need is to develop strength in your endo component; to slow down those hair-trigger reactions that jump in ahead, almost, of the event; to learn to let up, ease off, relax.

Tension and anxiety are always expressed in mind and body together, and releasing physical tensions immediately relieves anxiety (although the opposite is not always true; unconscious habits of physical tension may keep the muscles locked long after the "flight or fight" stimulus has passed).

• Your breathing is almost always tight. The breathing exercises on pages 141–143 will be helpful. And you have a particular spot where you tend to clutch: the solar plexus, that knot of nerve connections just below the breastbone, where you tighten under the stress of any sudden, strong emotion, especially fear and anger. Releasing at just that point, and in the belly below, calms and eases your whole body. Here's an exercise to develop awareness of that tension control center, so that you can release it as soon as you feel yourself grabbing hold there.

As in the breathing exercise on page 141, become aware of the breath entering and leaving your body; just let it move perfectly freely. Imagine that it enters and flows out through a hole in the lower part of your body, and on each movement of the breath think that your solar plexus is softening and spreading and dropping down into the floor. If you feel a knot of tightness there, think that it is slowly opening, undoing, separating, dissolving away. The more patiently you lightly send your awareness into that spot, the more sensitive you'll become to tightness there, your mind sifting down through deeper and deeper layers of tension, releasing each layer as it meets it. Let all of this happen on the slow, calm rhythm of your perfectly free breath.

Now feel the breath dropping deeper into your belly each time you relax for it to fall in, and relax again for it to fall out. Say to yourself, "My belly is soft, and dark, and quiet," as you imagine this peaceful center deep inside you. Do this for a few minutes, letting your mind drop deeper and deeper inside, with the breath, as you imagine this silent space within.

With this exercise you're establishing an inner center of peace and stillness, a refuge from overexposure to external stress, a place you can retreat to without losing contact with the outer world. You don't have to withdraw completely, as in sleep; you can go through this exercise any time, anywhere, with just a few moments of thought, putting your mind inside your body. Then you can return to whatever you're doing, refreshed and restored. Gradually, as you become more familiar and comfortable with the experience, you'll learn to incorporate some of that peacefulness and calm into your daily life.

Food: Undereaters Anonymous

Your eating habits vividly illustrate the precept that it's stress that brings out our innermost selves. Under stress, endos run to the refrigerator. An unhappy love affair or a setback at work is almost a guarantee of weight gain. You're just the opposite: Under stress you can't eat. Those fine meso ecto bones look sharper and sharper, the longer you're unhappy. Just when you need most to keep your strength up is when it's hardest for you to do it. Food repels you at such times, and you have to force yourself to eat. Surprisingly, you're as ashamed of your inability to get the food down as endos are when they're out of control in the other direction.

- Follow the guidelines for balanced ectos (see pages 159– 160).

- *Regular* mealtimes are especially important for you; if you wait too long to eat, you find you can't. Unlike endos, who get hungrier and hungrier and then fill up when the food arrives, the longer you wait to eat the less you can eat. It's as though your stomach clamps tight at the stress even of hunger.

- Make your surroundings at mealtime as harmonious and pleasant as possible; tension stress always affects your stomach, cuts your appetite, and you can't afford to miss meals.

• Strike a balance between protein and carbohydrates; get plenty of the latter. This is especially valuable at night, for carbohydrates will help to relax you. If like many meso ectos you're an insomniac—and under stress, sleep is even more difficult for you than eating—try a high-carbohydrate, high-calorie minimeal before bedtime, featuring pasta, noodles, bread, or pancakes. You're less likely to be troubled by digestive problems at night, too; you tend to absorb calories more easily at the end of the day.

• Exercise, especially aerobics, will also help you relax. People who exercise regularly sleep better, feel better generally. And exercise normalizes the appetite in both directions: While it cuts endo appetites, it will stimulate yours. Just don't overdo it and burn off more than you take in.

Exercise: Running Free

• Any fitness program for you should alternate sports that take advantage of your ecto and meso strengths, such as running (virtually all champion runners are meso ectos), tennis, squash, and those that encourage endo, such as yoga, meditation and relaxation techniques, and such disciplines as tai chi, which through a series of flowing movements teaches tranquillity, flexibility, and harmony of mind and body.

• A tip to use in any aerobic activity: As it intensifies, expel your breath more forcefully than you take it in. This keeps your ribs moving freely, ensures that you don't hold your breath, helps increase your lung capacity. Most people think the problem is inhaling enough air, whereas it's usually letting enough out; if you exhale vigorously enough, the inrush of breath occurs naturally, and in greater volume.

• At least twice a week be sure to include calisthenics that emphasize stretching. Always stretch slowly, to the limit of elasticity; never try to force beyond it, and don't bounce. Move only on the outgoing breath (as described on pages 144–145); think that it's the breath that moves your body.

- To build muscle strength and endurance, try the weight
  training program described on pages 126–127. Go slowly,
  and *always* take the weight through the entire range of
  movement. Keep the movement smooth; don't stop in a
  locked position for a rest. When in doubt, do less: lower
  weights, fewer reps. You're quite susceptible to injury from
  workouts that are too intense. *Take your time*: a rule of life for
  meso ectos.

POSTSCRIPT

By now you can see how a knowledge of body types will tell you not only who you are, but how an understanding of who you are, of your inner self, can release the untapped power within you for developing that self to its fullest potential.

There is a widespread conviction in our mass consumer society that we can all be "conditioned" by outside forces—whether they be parents, teachers, employers, politicians, or advertisers—in any direction they choose; that under the right circumstances we can be programmed and reprogrammed to suit other people's convenience, meet other people's expectations, whatever those may be. A knowledge of body types shows us that on the contrary, there is a bedrock of being in each one of us—a biological soul—that refuses to be manipulated, that follows its own laws.

But an understanding of body types also can mean just the opposite: a liberation from the prison of self. To realize that your habitual response to any given situation is not inevitable, but one among many possible responses, depending upon your constitutional makeup, has the paradoxical effect of giving you more choices. For it shows you, first of all, that it is not only what's out there that's determining your response to it, but that an inner predisposition is also at work, and that the world looks very different to those who are structurally and temperamentally different from you.

What's still more important, though, is that focusing upon your inner self directs your energies toward those components of structure and personality that may not at present be active in your life—that need to be developed. Understanding body types gives you a framework for growth.

And most important of all—it puts the power for change in *your* hands.

What your body type tells you about yourself can mean a happier, more productive life, with no dead ends—one in which you can fulfill your possible dreams. Most of us only dimly and intermittently perceive who we really are. We have brief moments of well-being, flashes in which we suddenly realize, "*This* is where I ought to be, this is what I should be doing," but too often we don't know just what it was that felt so right, or how to recapture it and make it part of our life.

So we let the moment slip away, like all the other moments that spoke for an instant, telling us we'd seen a better way, one that was truer to our inmost self—if only we knew how to read the message.

The message is in our own bodies.

It is the hope of this book that it will start you on a lifelong adventure of self-discovery.